Praise!

Praise!

A Door to God's Presence

RUTH AND WARREN MYERS

CLC PUBLICATIONS
Fort Washington, PA 19034

Praise: A Door to God's Presence

Published by CLC Publications

USA: P.O. Box 1449, Fort Washington, PA 19034
www.clcpublications.com

UK: Kingsway CLC Trust, Unit 5, Glendale Avenue, Sandycroft, Flintshire, CH5 2QP
www.equippingthechurch.com

Library of Congress Catalog No. 87-62359

This CLC edition published 2023

Printed in the United States of America

ISBN-13 (paperback): 978-1-61958-386-3

ISBN-13 (e-book): 978-1-61958-389-4

Italics in Scripture quotations are the emphasis of the author.

Contents

PART III: FREEDOM

Foreword

SOME BOOKS ARE TO be read and laid aside. Others are worth reading and rereading. *Praise!: A Door to God's Presence* falls into the latter category. The vital themes of worship, praise, and thanksgiving are presented with thoughtful research, warm devotion, and practical instruction.

These three elements are not optional extras but are basic to a life that brings glory to God and spiritual maturity to the worshipper. Too often our prayers are man-centered, whereas in His pattern prayer our Lord clearly taught that God and His glory should have precedence over man and his needs. It is in the act and attitude of worship that God communicates His presence to us.

The authors have made the whole of Scripture tributary to their purpose. The book is a shining example of the way Scripture can be used to fuel the fires of love and devotion, and enrich the whole of life. Most of the great worship passages of the Bible are woven into the text. Problems that arise in prayer are considered. For example, the exhortation to "always give thanks for everything," which seems a counsel of perfection, is satisfyingly answered.

The chapter on corporate worship and praise—a matter of great debate in our day—is replete with suggestions that should help make this important exercise more profitable and vital. The concluding section, which gives suggestions for seven days of praise, is helpful and should stimulate the reader to follow the same pattern.

The authors' suggestion that the book be read a chapter a week—and then practiced throughout the week—will return rich spiritual dividends.

— J. Oswald Sanders

Preface

Rewards and Dangers

ONE MORNING WE were discussing with friends the value of praising God continually and thanking Him for all things. Their son, a young college professor, quietly remarked, "Thanking and praising God for everything—that could open a Pandora's Box." His words especially caught Ruth's attention. For days questions tumbled through her mind: Can praise and thanksgiving be dangerous or unscriptural? How might they resemble the magical box that, when opened, loosed a chain of harmful consequences?

Dangers and Misconceptions

As we reflected on God's Word and on various praise practices, we began to see more clearly the importance of anchoring thanksgiving and praise in an accurate knowledge of God and His Word. On this foundation they can become the outflow of genuine worship in which we offer to the Lord ourselves as well as our appreciation. In this context, praise and thanksgiving can become a source of delight. They can strengthen us and provide us with a unique way to bring glory and pleasure to God. But without scriptural perspectives and guidelines, praise can indeed open a Pandora's Box of results that do not glorify God.

Here are a few of these harmful results. Unreal Christians with smiling masks and repressed emotions. Unyielded Christians who, through praise, hope to maneuver God into doing what they wish.

Confused Christians who believe that God causes trials that they in fact bring on themselves. Passive Christians who use praise as a substitute for seeking intelligent solutions for life's problems. And resentful Christians who blame God for not rewarding their praise with trouble-free lives.

If we view praise as a cure for every ailment and the primary secret of success in the Christian life, we are likely to neglect other essentials—prayer for ourselves and others, diligent intake of God's Word, and daily obedience to Christ as Lord. If we place too much emphasis on the emotional aspects of praise, we become disillusioned when we reach one of life's emotionally dry periods. Or we discourage sincere believers who seldom experience strong emotions as they praise, making them think they will never be able to develop an acceptable praise life. Yet if we fear and avoid emotions in our praise, we miss much of the enjoyment and many of the benefits that can be ours.

Many Christians neglect praise entirely or consign it to the fringes of their lives. Some are preoccupied with other interests or plagued with questions about praise. Others cannot reconcile the nature of God with His desire for praise and worship. In their minds, asking for praise conveys the impression of a vain or insecure person who craves admiration, much as a teenager may crave compliments or a celebrity applause. Still others stumble because they do not understand the scriptural background for giving thanks regardless of what happens to them.

Rewards

Again and again in the Bible we find people praising and thanking the Lord and instructing others to do the same:

> Offer to God a sacrifice of thanksgiving. (Ps. 50:14)
>
> Praise the Lord!
> Praise Him, O servants of the Lord. (135:1)

> You who revere the Lord, bless the Lord. (135:20)
>
> In everything give thanks; for this is God's will for you in Christ Jesus. (1 Thess. 5:18)
>
> Through Him then let us continually offer up a sacrifice of praise to God. (Heb. 13:15)

God places great importance on worship, praise, and thanksgiving. He does so not because He is an egotist with selfish desires but because He has our best interests at heart. Praise and thanksgiving help us rise above self-centeredness to Christ-centeredness. They focus our hearts and minds on the Lord and make us more like Him. We cheat ourselves when we neglect them, for they are a tonic that promotes joy and spiritual vigor.

Besides its effect on our inner life, praise enables God to give us external deliverances and blessings, which in turn call forth fresh praise.

Withholding praise and thanksgiving is an injustice toward God. We owe Him everything, and it is only right that we give thanks to Him and ascribe to Him "the glory due to His name" (Ps. 29:2).

PRAISE ENABLES GOD TO GIVE US EXTERNAL DELIVERANCES AND BLESSINGS, WHICH IN TURN CALL FORTH FRESH PRAISE.

For these reasons and many others, worship expressed in praise and thanksgiving is not a mere obligation. It is one of our greatest privileges as children of the living God. It should rank high in our priorities.

As we learn biblical principles and develop our ability to appreciate and adore the Lord, worship, praise, and thanksgiving can become supremely gratifying. C.S. Lewis wrote regarding praise:

> I think we delight to praise what we enjoy because the praise not merely expresses but completes the enjoyment; it is its appointed consummation. It is not out of compliment that lovers keep on telling one another how beautiful they are; the delight is incomplete till it is expressed. It is frustrating to have discovered a new author and not to be able to tell anyone how good he is; to come suddenly, at the turn of the road, upon some mountain valley of unexpected grandeur and then to have to keep silent because the people with you care for it no more than for a tin can in the ditch; to hear a good joke and find no one to share it with (the perfect hearer died a year ago). This is so even when our expressions are inadequate, as of course they usually are. But how if one could really and fully praise even such things to perfection—utterly "get out" in poetry or music or paint the upsurge of appreciation which almost bursts you? Then indeed the object would be fully appreciated and our delight would have attained perfect development. The worthier the object, the more intense this delight would be. If it were possible for a created soul fully (I mean, up to the full measure conceivable in a finite being) to "appreciate," that is to love and delight in, the worthiest object of all, and simultaneously at every moment to give this delight perfect expression, then that soul would be in supreme beatitude.[1]

Our prayer is that this book will lead you into increased delight in the worthiest Object of all and into a more constant, more joyful expression of that delight.

1 C.S. Lewis, *Reflections on the Psalms* (London: Collins, 1967), 81.

Part I

Foundations

As a gold field gives up its treasures to those who search for them, so the Bible yields rich reasons to get excited about God to those who seek to know Him better.

In our praise we can never exhaust the splendor of our majestic and merciful God. As our knowledge of Him deepens, we realize that He is, in the words of A. W. Tozer, "utterly and completely delightful . . . the most winsome of all beings."

The following chapters can enrich your worship by helping you develop a clearer focus on God, a renewed surrender to Christ as Lord, and a fuller experience of the Holy Spirit.

1

Focusing on God

ONE EVENING IN BOMBAY I was traveling north from the Gateway of India to meet Warren at our guest house. Suddenly a breathtaking display captured my attention. God was treating me to one of His extravaganzas, illuminating the entire western sky out over the Indian Ocean. Blind to historical buildings and frenetic traffic, my eyes feasted on the brilliant strata of rubies and corals stroked with accents of luminous white and pale blue. The colors danced for joy until at last they settled down in a bed of crimson embers, blanketed with silver ash.

Faith and Praise

We can enjoy sunsets because God has given us the faculty of sight. The same ability lets us experience the greenness of grass and the wonder on a child's face. Just as sight is a physical faculty, so faith is a spiritual one that lets our inner eyes see God. Faith is basic to God's work in our lives. Through it we experience Him, first in the new birth and then with increasing appreciation as we grow spiritually. Faith begins when we respond to God as He has revealed Himself in Christ. It matures as we continue to learn more of Him.

Faith is looking to the Lord to take action on our behalf. It is depending on Him to provide and protect, to satisfy and empower. Faith is believing that what God has said is true and that what He has promised He will do.

At first, many of us look to the Lord with a degree of uncertainty. As our faith becomes stronger, we depend on Him with increased confidence. Our faith begins to resemble the settled expectancy that Abraham experienced:

> He did not waver in unbelief, but grew strong in faith, giving glory to God, and being fully assured that what He had promised, He was able also to perform. (Rom. 4:20–21)

Praise, like faith, means focusing on God. Faith is looking to God with trust; praise is looking at God with admiration. Faith is the root from which our praise develops, and praise in turn strengthens our faith. The step between admiring God and trusting Him is a small one.

> **Faith is the root from which our praise develops, and praise in turn strengthens our faith.**

Again and again Ruth and I find praise a quick route from merely trying to believe God to trusting Him with a settled confidence. In a variety of ways, we slide off the highway of faith. One is through feeling frustrated at unfinished paperwork and people work, coupled with regret about neglecting something important.

One night we were walking along the beach that borders the Singapore harbor, praying together. Suddenly I remembered an urgent letter I had procrastinated in writing. As I lamented my delay, Ruth joined my mood, embellishing it with anxiety about the problems this might cause the couple to whom we owed the letter.

After our morbid side trip, we got back to prayer. We praised God for His sovereignty, His unlimited power, and His promises to work on our behalf. We asked Him to overrule my negligence and use the situation for good. Praise helped us fix our faith on God, who is greater than our failures, greater than our responsibilities, greater than our spiritual enemy who loves to accuse and discourage us.

Though we chose to praise with tiny stirrings of faith, God released us from our unbelief and renewed our confidence in Him. Praise became a ramp onto the freeway of faith. Weeks later our friends wrote, "We would not have been ready for your suggestions a week earlier." God had used the delay to get the letter to its destination at just the right time.

Looking at God

The secret of both faith and praise is a growing knowledge of God. Meditating day after day on His perfect character and magnificence inspires us to trust Him and praise Him. Even as our hearts respond in awe to a sunset, so they respond in adoration when our inner eyes see the Lord as He truly is. The more we look and worship, the more God sensitizes us to His presence so that He becomes more real and dear to us than anyone on earth.

Both individually and as a couple, we often use Psalm 145 for praise and prayer. This psalm is one of the greatest praise chapters in the Bible. It declares that God is highly to be praised because of His awesome greatness and His abundant goodness.

God is both strong and tender. On the one hand, He is full of splendor and majesty, performing wonderful deeds and ruling over a glorious Kingdom that will endure forever. On the other hand, He is full of grace, mercy, and lovingkindness. In Him, strength blends with gentleness, righteousness with kindness, and mighty victories with the constant provision of our tiniest needs. He is majestic and exalted, yet near to all who call on Him in truth. He cares intensely about us and fulfills our desires as we fear Him.

What an astounding blend of qualities we find in God! This reminds us of the advertisements entitled, "Tough, but oh, so gentle," which pictured a burly, muscular man feeding a baby or cuddling a kitten. Our God offers us tender care and strong protection. He knows when we need gentle love and when we need tough love. He is awesome yet welcoming, majestic yet knowable.

The New Testament adds yet another dimension to our praise. Revelation 5:12 says, "Worthy is the Lamb that was slain to receive power and riches and wisdom and might and honor and glory and blessing." When Jesus died for us, the crushing weight of all our sin fell on Him. As a result, we who trust Him can enjoy glorious liberty as children of our almighty, all-loving, altogether desirable God. What praise and honor He deserves!

Extolling and Magnifying God

How delightful it can be to honor God by praise! We read in Psalm 147:1: "Praise the Lord! For it is good to sing praises to our God; for it is pleasant and praise is becoming." Praise was never meant to be an irksome responsibility. True, it is often a costly sacrifice, requiring a radical choice against busyness or contrary emotions.

We do not find it easy to postpone pressing or enticing activities to include adequate praise in our quiet times. Nor do we find it easy to take our hearts in hand and praise the Lord when we feel tense with anxiety or want to enjoy the luxury of complaints or angry mental arguments. Yet when we choose against ourselves (or is it really choosing *for* ourselves?) and begin to praise, we discover anew how liberating and uplifting praise is.

Many words in the Bible enlarge our sense of what praise involves. To praise is to *bless*, *honor*, and *glorify* the Lord. It is to speak of His wonders and boast of Him. It is to stand in awe of Him and glory in who He is. Praise often includes singing, or even shouting, for joy and gladness. Psalm 145:7 says, "They shall eagerly utter [bubble over with, celebrate] the memory of Thine abundant goodness." We praise God not only when we speak directly to Him but also when we tell others our high view of Him. Whether directed to the Lord or to other people, whether expressed with outer exuberance or quiet enjoyment, praise includes adoring God for who He is and appreciating what He does.

After the Exodus from Egypt the ancient Israelites praised the Lord with an excited sense of appreciation and adoration. Overwhelmed at His lovingkindness and glorious strength, they rehearsed how He had led them safely through the Red Sea and then drowned the entire Egyptian army which pursued them. They exclaimed:

> Who among the gods is like you, O Lord?
> Who is like you—majestic in holiness,
> Awesome in glory, working wonders? (Exod. 15:11)

Some years ago a young hippie was sitting on a park bench reading the account of the Red Sea victory. Suddenly he began to shout, "Hallelujah! Praise the Lord! What a miracle! Hallelujah!"

A distinguished-looking agnostic stopped to ask the reason for his unseemly exuberance. The hippie replied, "I was just reading how God parted the Red Sea and the whole nation of Israel walked through it on dry ground, and I just couldn't help saying, 'Hallelujah! What a miracle!'"

"But my dear young man, don't you know that it was not a real sea at all, but just a few inches of water in a marsh?" After delivering this rebuttal the agnostic turned and walked on, leaving behind a confused and disheartened young Christian.

But soon hallelujahs again pierced the air. Irritated, the agnostic returned and asked, "Now what are you shouting about?"

"Well, sir, I just read how God drowned the whole Egyptian army in a few inches of water. What a miracle! Hallelujah! Praise the Lord!"

With or Without Pleasant Emotions

At times you may feel as excited as this young man about our God of limitless power and love. Such excitement is appropriate. But refuse to measure the success of your praise and worship by how you feel. If nothing happens in your feelings, do not give up. Give God a chance to develop your spiritual responses by regularly meditating on His Word and persisting in praise.

We should be grateful for the elated moments or hours when we sense God's presence, yet not expect such feelings to be continuous. Sometimes God uses mountaintop experiences to exhilarate and reassure us. Through them He transforms our outlook and refreshes our sense of life's meaning. We can nourish our hearts by remembering such times, but we must not feel they are God's will for us continually. Our Lord Jesus experienced the Mount of Transfiguration; He also experienced Gethsemane and Mount Calvary. Life includes dusty roads and dismal mists as well as the highlands of elation.

GIVE GOD A CHANCE TO DEVELOP YOUR SPIRITUAL RESPONSES BY REGULARLY MEDITATING ON HIS WORD AND PERSISTING IN PRAISE.

Though we cannot always pray or praise with the same emotional satisfaction, we can always pray and praise in ways that please God. The helpful booklet *Quiet Time* encourages us to concentrate on giving rather than getting when we worship and to persist whether or not we feel blessed and refreshed:

God is seeking for men and women who will worship . . . Let us believe that Christ and His atoning death are worthy of everlasting praise and adoration, whether we actually derive any conscious benefit or not. Let us keep our eyes off ourselves and our own subjective experience, and keep them fixed by faith in worship and wonder on the Lord Jesus and Him crucified. God will see to it that we are blessed thereby, for "them that honour Me," He has said, "I will honour."[1]

Growing in Our Knowledge of God

Both of us constantly discover fresh passages that stimulate us to praise or we renew our friendship with special verses we have memorized in the past. Several of our favorites were penned by the prophet Jeremiah:

> There is none like Thee, O Lord;
> Thou art great, and great is Thy name in might.
> Who would not fear Thee, O King of the nations?
> Indeed it is Thy due!
> For among all the wise men of the nations
> And in all their kingdoms,
> There is none like Thee. (Jer. 10:6–7)
>
> But the Lord is the true God;
> He is the living God and the everlasting King.
> At His wrath the earth quakes,
> And the nations cannot endure His indignation.
> . . . .
> It is He who made the earth by His power,
> Who established the world by His wisdom;
> And by His understanding He has stretched out the heavens.
> (10:10, 12)
>
> Ah Lord God! Behold, Thou hast made the heavens and the earth by Thy great power and by Thine outstretched arm! Nothing is too difficult for Thee. (32:17)

---

1 *Quiet Time* (Downers Grove, IL: InterVarsity Press, 1945), 5–6.

In our praise we can never exhaust the splendor of our incomparable God. As our knowledge of Him deepens, we realize that He is "utterly and completely delightful . . . the most winsome of all beings."[2] More and more, praise becomes our crowning activity, a delight to our heart. This was the experience of the old man who wrote Psalm 71. This psalmist faced life with increasing praise and deep confidence, for he knew who God was and asked Him to be that to him personally in the midst of his present troubles and distresses:

> Be Thou to me a rock of habitation, to which I may
> continually come.
> For Thou art my rock and my fortress.
> . . . .
> Thou art my hope;
> O Lord GOD, Thou art my confidence.
> By Thee I have been sustained from my birth;
> Thou art He who took me from my mother's womb;
> My praise is continually of Thee.
> . . . .
> I will hope continually,
> And will praise Thee yet more and more.
> (Ps. 71:3, 5–6, 14)

After years of walking with God, this man continued to grow in praise.

Regardless of how far we have progressed spiritually, to keep our praise from stagnating we must freshen it daily with a deepening knowledge of God. We must press on to know Him better, "finding still fresh material for praise beyond all past praises."[3] Then, even when we are distressed by trials, we can

---

2 A.W. Tozer, *The Root of the Righteous* (Harrisburg, PA: Christian Publications, Inc., 1955), 15.

3 William Wilson, *Wilson's Old Testament Word Studies* (McLean, VA: MacDonald Publishing Company, 1980), 322.

focus on Him and "greatly rejoice with joy inexpressible and full of glory" (1 Pet. 1:8).

For Personal Meditation and Group Discussion

1. From both the Preface and Chapter 1, list three or more reasons why it is important to magnify God through worship, praise, and thanksgiving.
2. What is the relationship between praise and faith?
3. What truths stand out to you about praise? About God?

2

Experiencing God's Power and Presence

TO ESCAPE FROM PRESSURES or boredom, some people spend every leisure moment cruising social media, streaming a movie, or listening to music. In moderation such diversions are helpful. But God offers us a vastly superior solution to our emptiness and problems. Anywhere, anytime, we can tune in to His presence, feast our eyes on His beauty or rest our hearts in His sufficiency. Without expensive equipment or even earphones, we can experience relaxation and renewal through praise.

Praise—Not Optional, but Essential

With its great potential for enriching our experience of God, what place does praise occupy in our daily lives? Do we praise God consistently or just occasionally when prompted by spurts of gratitude? Do we enjoy praise or do we endure it as a duty that we hope will guarantee God's blessing?

Some Christians are skeptical about praise because of uncomfortable encounters with praise enthusiasts who lack discretion. Others miss out on its blessings through secular, or even spiritual, busyness. If we want to love God with all our hearts and fully enjoy the resources He offers us, we cannot neglect praise. Praise is not optional, but essential.

Praise both demonstrates and develops faith, and faith brings power—power that changes our circumstances, power that changes us. Faith enables us to obey God and to achieve success in His eyes, as did His people of old. In Hebrews 11 we read that by faith they "conquered kingdoms, performed acts of righteousness, obtained promises, shut the mouths of lions, quenched the power of fire, escaped the edge of the sword, from weakness were made strong" (Heb. 11:33–34). By faith they also honored God when they were failures from the world's point of view. For Christ's sake, they were destitute, afflicted, ill-treated, tortured, imprisoned, killed. In our lives, as in theirs, adversities as well as achievements can be victories for God if by faith we do His will. And praise helps to stimulate our faith.

Experiencing God's Power

Prayer has been called the slender nerve that moves the mighty hand of God. This is especially true of prayer blended with praise. It brings us God's blessings in ways we otherwise miss. It focuses our eyes on God, and He in turn focuses His power and lovingkindness on our lives and situations.

Second Chronicles 20 dramatizes the value of prayer that is filled with praise and faith. An alliance of three powerful armies had converged on the little kingdom of Judah. When news of the attack reached King Jehoshaphat, he trembled with fear. Then in desperation he turned his attention to God and prayed for deliverance, saturating his prayer with praise. He began by extolling God as exalted and invincible:

> O Lord, the God of our fathers, art Thou not God in the heavens? And art Thou not ruler over all the kingdoms of the nations? Power and might are in Thy hand so that no one can stand against Thee. (2 Chron. 20:6)

Then he added further praise for past victories God had wrought and for promises He had given.

Having glorified God and rekindled his faith through praise, King Jehoshaphat briefly rehearsed his distress to the Lord. He said, "We are powerless before this great multitude who are coming against us; nor do we know what to do, but our eyes are on Thee" (2 Chron. 20:12). God replied through His prophet, "Do not fear or be dismayed because of this great multitude, for the battle is not yours but God's" (2 Chron. 20:15). What was Jehoshaphat's response? More worship and praise.

PRAISE FOCUSES OUR EYES ON GOD, AND HE IN TURN FOCUSES HIS POWER AND LOVING KINDNESS ON OUR LIVES AND SITUATIONS.

The next day, by faith in God and His promise, Jehoshaphat's army marched to the battlefield in an unusual battle formation. The choir, robes and all, led the attack! And when they began to sing and to praise, the Lord caused the three enemy armies to fight among themselves until they annihilated each other. Not one enemy soldier survived.

After the victory, it took three days for God's people to take home all the treasures they found in the enemy camp. And the kingdom of Judah enjoyed peace for the rest of Jehoshaphat's reign. God used this traumatic situation for good, bringing victory and enrichment. What were the keys that moved His mighty hand? Much praise, a simple request, faith in God's Word, then worship and more praise as a sign of that faith. As in an earlier battle during the reign of Jehoshaphat's grandfather, "The sons of Judah *conquered because they trusted* in the LORD" (2 Chron. 13:18).

Experiencing God's Presence

Through praise we can enhance our experience of God's presence as well as His power. At the dedication of Solomon's temple, "When they praised the LORD . . . the glory of the LORD filled the house of God" (2 Chron. 5:13–14). Psalm 22:3 tells us that God "inhabits" (KJV) or is "enthroned upon" (NASB) the praises of His people. His presence is always in us and with us as His living temples, much as television waves surround us, whether we tune in to them or not.

As we express and strengthen our faith through praise, we enthrone God in our situation. We tune ourselves in to enjoy His sovereign sufficiency. God in turn manifests His presence on our behalf, in both inner and outer ways. He uses our trials as a stage on which He displays His love and power and faithfulness. As a result, His reality becomes evident both to us and to others who observe our lives.

In 1960 when my first husband, Dean Denler, was hospitalized with terminal cancer, praise took on new importance in his life. He told me that he would be praising God for all eternity, but only here on earth could he bring joy to God's heart by praising Him in the midst of pain. So Dean decided to make his hospital room a special dwelling place for God through praise. Officiating at his funeral some months later, a close friend said, "His room became a sanctuary, his bed a pulpit, and all who came to comfort him were blessed." Praise did not bring healing of the cancer. But through praise and faith Dean brought the refreshment of God's presence into a painful situation, honoring God in death as he had in life.

Whether in life or death, whether in times of blessing or times of suffering, the God who rules over all creation wants to manifest His presence on our behalf. His presence is powerful. It overwhelms His enemies and makes satanic powers tremble. His presence is majestic and awe-inspiring, full of glory, gladness, and strength. His presence is with us at all times. But as we praise Him by faith, we learn to enjoy His all-sufficient presence in new ways.

> **AS WE PRAISE HIM, HE REINFORCES OUR HUMANNESS WITH INNER STRENGTH THROUGH HIS SPIRIT, MAKING US SUPERMEN AND SUPERWOMEN IN THE SPIRITUAL REALM.**

How much we should praise the Lord for the lavish blessings His presence provides! He is within us as living water (John 7:38), above us as protecting shade (Ps. 57:1), and underneath us with His everlasting arms (Deut. 33:27). He goes before us as our Shepherd to guide us and to prepare our circumstances (John 10:4). He follows behind us as our rear guard to defend us and smooth over our mistakes (Isa. 52:12). He walks beside us as our dearest Friend, holding our right hand and saying, "Fear not, I will help you" (41:13). Even when we distrust Him and stumble, He is there holding us up and keeping us from falling headlong (Ps. 37:24). He is ready to chasten us as necessary and always eager to restore us. As we praise Him, He reinforces our humanness with inner strength through His Spirit, making us supermen and superwomen in the spiritual realm.

How can we help but agree with Psalm 73:25–26?

> Whom have I in heaven but Thee?
> And besides Thee, I desire nothing on earth.
>
> My flesh and my heart may fail;
> But God is the strength of my heart and my portion forever.

How can we help but respond to God as Moses did in Exodus 33:15, when he prayed, "If Thy presence does not go with us, do not lead us up from here." He preferred to abandon the great venture he was leading rather than proceed without God's presence.

Why do we often proceed without God's evident presence in our lives and ventures? A basic reason could be our failure to praise and worship the Lord. C.S. Lewis went through a period when he was beset with misunderstanding about why praise is important. Later he wrote:

> I did not see that it is in the process of being worshiped that God communicates His presence to men. It is not indeed the only way. But for many people at many times, the "fair beauty of the Lord" is revealed chiefly or only while they worship Him together.[1]

Through our worship and praise, both with others and in private, we can enthrone God in our situations and make our surroundings His special dwelling place. Praise can become the switch that turns on the light and power of His presence. It helps us say "yes" to life in all its fullness.

For Personal Meditation and Group Discussion

1. What benefits mentioned in this chapter especially motivate you to praise?
2. What did you learn about praise from the examples given?
3. Can you think of any need or situation in your life, large or small, in which you could begin praising God daily?

---

1 C.S. Lewis, *Reflections on the Psalms* (London: Collins, 1967), 79.

3

Worshipping in Spirit and in Truth

AS STEREO MUSIC involves richness of sound, so worship, praise, and thanksgiving produce a three-dimensional fullness in our response to God. Through them we minister directly to the Lord Himself, whereas through serving people we minister to Him indirectly.

To praise and thank God appropriately we must worship Him. In worship we humble ourselves before God in reverent submission and lift our hearts to Him in adoration. Worship can be vocal or silent. It can be alone or with others, whether two or three or a thousand. It can include outer expressions such as bowing down, kneeling, or lifting our hands. But the essential core of worship is centering our hearts on God.

Responding in Spirit

In the Old Testament, God chose the Temple at Jerusalem as the place where He would dwell in a unique way. There He manifested His glory. There, through rituals He had prescribed, His people worshipped Him.

Jesus announced a radical change. Resting by Jacob's well after a long journey by foot, He began talking with a Samaritan woman. When she brought up the subject of where to worship, He broke the revolutionary news: the external place was no longer important. Then He revealed the secret of true worship:

> The hour is coming, and now is, when the true worshipers will worship the Father in spirit and truth; for the Father is seeking such to worship Him. God is Spirit, and those who worship Him must worship in spirit and truth (John 4:23–24, NKJV).

Jesus wants us to realize that worship is an inner spiritual response, not just an outward expression or form. It must come from our spirit, the innermost essence of our person. It is not dependent on externals—a prescribed place, beautiful surroundings, familiar rituals, inspiring music, or specific bodily movements.

> **WORSHIP IS AN INNER SPIRITUAL RESPONSE, NOT JUST AN OUTWARD EXPRESSION OR FORM.**

Externals are not wrong. But they are not essential to worship, nor are we to depend on them. We can worship when the slightest sound would awaken the baby. We can worship in the frenetic rush of a city street, in the bustling dignity of a modern office, or in the solitary confinement of a prison. Externals of any kind are not necessary. With or without them, we may worship the Father "in spirit."

God's Superlative Gift

The paragraphs preceding John 4:23 throw light on what it means to worship in spirit. If our spirit is dead, estranged from God and His life, we cannot worship. Only by being born of His Spirit does our spirit become alive to the living God. This happens when, by faith in Jesus as our Savior and Lord, we first drink the water of life that He freely offers. Then the living water of God's Spirit becomes in us a fountain that can spring up into a vital experience of eternal, abundant life.

A spring or an artesian well gushes forth water because it is connected to vast underground reserves of water. An ornamental fountain springs up because it is connected to the city reservoir. By giving us His Spirit, our heavenly Father has connected us with Himself and His infinite, abundant life. He has linked us with His resources, which can supply every imaginable need: strength, righteousness, love, hope, wisdom, and thankfulness, as well as special grace to obey Him in every relationship and responsibility. When we depend on Him as our rich and full supply, the fountain of God's Spirit springs up in us. It flushes out impurities, revives and refreshes us, and overflows as a life-giving stream to others (John 7:37–38). The flow increases as we learn to depend on God more fully.

The illustration of living water springing up within us is Jesus' description of being filled with the Spirit. Being Spirit-filled is not a complicated achievement. It is a simple and sincere relating to our wonderful God and His Son as we allow His Spirit to reveal Them to us. It happens as we yield to the Holy Spirit in simple faith and choose to obey God's Word by His power. Being filled results in vital worship and growing Christlikeness.

In John 6:63 Jesus said, "It is the Spirit who gives life; the flesh profits nothing; the words that I have spoken to you are spirit and are life." From the beginning to the end of our spiritual sojourn, life comes from the Spirit of the Lord in conjunction with the Word of the Lord. The Spirit imparts life and power for our soul's enrichment, for our spiritual growth, for our service and for our worship.

Jesus said that the flesh, in contrast to the life-giving Spirit, profits nothing. If we are filled with ourselves (with our human perspective and human ways and human abilities) instead of with the Spirit, we offer God dead works and dead worship. Our natural adequacy profits nothing. Nor can we store up spiritual adequacy over the years until ultimately we can operate without conscious dependence on the Holy Spirit. Always it is the Spirit who gives life and empowering as we depend on Him. Because He dwells in our spirit, we can worship God in spirit.

If we have not received spiritual life, or if we are out of fellowship with God, we cannot worship God as He desires. We may speak inspiring words, think illuminating thoughts, go through various externals, and even feel enthusiastic, but we cannot offer God acceptable worship. We can worship in spirit only as our spirit fellowships with God through His Spirit.

Worshipping in Truth

We must also worship in truth. We are not to be like the Samaritans in Jesus' day, who worshipped without knowing what they worshipped (John 4:22). But what does it mean to worship in truth?

The word translated "truth" in the Old Testament is closely related to the Hebrew words for pillar and for peg. This implies that truth is a strong, reliable support. In the New Testament Jesus said to the Father, "Your word is truth" (John 17:17, NIV). God's Word is absolute truth because He Himself is utterly true, faithful, and unchanging. His Word is dependable. It reveals God and life accurately. There is no discrepancy between what God says and what life is like, or between what God promises and what He does.

God has revealed truth most clearly through His written Word and through His Son, the living Word. Jesus said to His disciples, "I am the truth." Each of us began to make God's truth part of our inner person when we first received Christ. As we live in fellowship with Him and continue in His Word, letting the Holy Spirit teach us, we increasingly know the truth. And the truth sets us free—free from sin which clouds our fellowship with God, free from misconceptions about God which hinder our worship.

Because the Word reveals the true and living God, it prepares us to worship Him in truth, as He is. It delivers us from worshipping our vague or distorted mental images of Him.

God's Word becomes part of our thinking and living as we daily take it in and absorb it. This enables us to experience reality and stability in our inner life, in our worship, and in all that we do.

> **BECAUSE THE WORD REVEALS THE TRUE AND LIVING GOD, IT PREPARES US TO WORSHIP HIM IN TRUTH, AS HE IS.**

The Truths of the New Covenant

Worshipping in truth includes understanding the new covenant, which Jesus inaugurated. In the old covenant, sacrificial offerings were essential to approaching God. Some sacrifices had to do with homage and thanksgiving, but the heavy emphasis was on atoning for sin and securing God's goodwill. The sacrifices, which were constantly repeated, pointed ahead to the cross, which alone could totally take away sin and guilt forever. All of these Old Testament rituals have been fulfilled in Christ: "By one sacrifice he has made perfect forever those who are being made holy" (Heb. 10:14, NIV).

Under the new covenant we no longer need to devote any attention to atoning for sin, securing God's goodwill, or retaining His favor. This has been wholly accomplished, once for all, by our Lord's death and resurrection. Through Him, by faith alone on our part, we are clean and righteous. Our Holy God looks on us with abundant favor, which we in no way earn. He accepts us forever because of what Christ has done for us. Believing these truths and treasuring them in our heart help us worship in truth.

Though we no longer offer ceremonial sacrifices, we can profit by keeping Christ's sacrifice on the cross prominent in our worship. Meditating on what it cost the Lord to bear our sins reminds us to glory not in ourselves but in Him alone. It calls forth deep appreciation. It keeps us mindful of the only true and living way into God's presence.

Many songs can help us glory in Christ and the Cross. "Beneath the Cross of Jesus" is one of our favorites:

> Beneath the cross of Jesus
> I fain would take my stand:
> the shadow of a mighty rock
> within a weary land,
> a home within the wilderness,
> a rest upon the way,
> from the burning of the noon-tide heat
> and the burden of the day.
>
> Upon the cross of Jesus
> mine eye at times can see
> the very dying form of One
> who suffered there for me;
> and from my smitten heart, with tears
> two wonders I confess—
> the wonders of His matchless love
> and my unworthiness.
>
> I take, O cross, thy shadow
> for my abiding place;
> I ask no other sunshine than
> the sunshine of His face,
> content to let the world go by
> to know no gain nor loss
> my sinful self my only shame
> my glory all the cross.[1]

1 Elizabeth C. Clephane, "Beneath the Cross of Jesus," from *Inspiring Hymns*, compiled by Alfred B. Smith (Grand Rapids: Singspiration, 1951), 57.

An equally important truth for enriching our worship is the resurrection and ascension of Christ. Apart from the Resurrection, the cross would have been earth's greatest tragedy. But we worship a living, ascended Savior. God wants us to realize how immeasurably great is His power which is at work in us who believe:

> That power is the same divine energy which was demonstrated in Christ when he raised him from the dead and gave him the place of highest honour in Heaven—a place that is infinitely superior to any command, authority, power or control, and which carries with it a name far beyond any name that could ever be used in this world or the world to come. God has placed everything under the power of Christ and has set him up as head of everything to the Church. (Eph. 1:20–22, PHI)

As we let the truths about our Lord's exalted life and power grip our hearts, they deeply affect our worship. They cause us to exult in His triumph and to offer grateful thanks for His resurrection power within us. They increase our wonder as we worship our Lord Jesus Christ, the Lamb of God, who shares the throne of the universe:

> To Him who sits on the throne, and to the Lamb, be blessing and honor and glory and dominion forever and ever. (Rev. 5:13)

The Truth of God's Holiness

Broadening our understanding of who God is can also help us to worship in truth. As the God of truth, He is also a Holy God, a God of absolute moral purity and burning righteousness, uncontaminated by evil or corruption of any kind.

Therefore, to worship in truth means to worship in awe and reverent fear of our Holy God. It means that we come with humility, ready to turn from any sin He may reveal to us and longing to show forth the beauty of His holiness in our daily lives.

How grateful we should be that our majestic God is holy and morally perfect, with no deficiency in His righteousness or His love. If His character had an evil side, how could we trust Him fully or worship Him without reservation? In awed wonder we can rejoice that we worship a Holy Father, a Holy Son, and a Holy Spirit—a totally Holy Triune God. One of the most universal hymns of the Church summarizes the wonder of His holiness:

> Holy, Holy, Holy! Lord God Almighty!
> Early in the morning our song shall rise to Thee;
> Holy, Holy, Holy! merciful and mighty!
> God in Three Persons, blessed Trinity![2]

The truths of God's Word deliver us from trusting in false approaches to God. They free us from inadequate concepts of God, which result in unacceptable worship. They help us to worship the Father in truth.

> **TO WORSHIP IN TRUTH MEANS TO WORSHIP IN AWE AND REVERENT FEAR OF OUR HOLY GOD.**

Responding with a True Heart

Worshipping in truth also involves inner personal truth: a genuine, truthful heart that is not hypocritical. Hebrews 10:22 exhorts us to draw near with a sincere heart, a true heart, a heart sprinkled clean from an evil conscience. Such a heart is not pretending. It does not profess a greater holiness of life than it has reached. Nor does it put up a false front by covering known sin, for it reveres the One who says, "He who conceals his transgressions will not prosper, but he who confesses and forsakes them will find compassion" (Prov. 28:13).

---

2 Reginald Heber, "Holy, Holy, Holy," from *Inspiring Hymns*, compiled by Alfred B. Smith, 20.

A true heart does not hide its weaknesses and mistakes. It may be wrestling with failure in certain areas, but it is honest with God about its struggles. It comes before Him with humility, admitting its deep need for help and further holiness.

A true heart does not postpone worship until it feels more deserving. This would be foolish, for beholding and worshipping God is part of His prescription for greater holiness. Beneath any surface struggles and defeats, a true heart maintains its deep inner alignment with the Lord's will. Its very struggles against sin and its distress at disobedience demonstrate that this basic alignment is still there. A true heart is loyal to Jesus as the one true Way. It comes before God by grace—by unmerited favor—and worships in His merits alone:

> Just as I am, without one plea,
> But that Thy blood was shed for me,
> And that Thou bid'st me come to Thee—
> O Lamb of God, I come, I come![3]

Worship opens us afresh to the Lord's work in us, hastening a growing commitment that can say:

> Just as I am, Thy love unknown
> Has broken every barrier down;
> Now to be Thine, yea, Thine alone,
> O Lamb of God, I come, I come![4]

If you feel you cannot honestly say this, you can turn it into a prayer, such as: "Father, I look to You, through Your compassionate love, to break down any barriers in my heart, known or unknown, so that in a new and lasting way I will be Yours and Yours alone." Then with a true and grateful heart, you can extol and honor Him.

---

3 Charlotte Elliott, "Just as I Am," from *Hymns* (Chicago: InterVarsity Press, 1960), 53.

4 Elliott, 53.

An Adventure in Reality

Worshipping in spirit and in truth includes far more than pleasant devotional feelings. It involves dangers as well as delights. Richard Foster wrote of worshipping in truth:

> Willard Sperry declared, "Worship is a deliberate and disciplined adventure in reality." It is not for the timid or comfortable. It involves an opening of ourselves to the dangerous life of the Spirit.[5]

True worship exposes us to the reality of God. This includes His tender love, but more. It includes the consuming fire of His powerful presence against sin in our lives; it includes the glare of His truth that discloses our comfortable delusions. It unveils the worthlessness of the idols we treasure in His rightful place. An unknown poet wrote:

> What has stripped the seeming beauty
> From the idols of the earth?
> Not a sense of right or duty,
> But the sight of peerless worth.
> Not the crushing of those idols
> With its bitter void and smart,
> But the beaming of His beauty,
> The unveiling of His heart.[6]

Worship is dangerous. Yet it is safe. It replaces what it consumes with something of surpassing worth.

---

5 Richard Foster, *Celebration of Discipline* (San Francisco: Harper and Row, 1978), 149.

6 "Peerless Worth," author and source unknown.

For Personal Meditation and Group Discussion

1. Summarize what it means to:

    a. worship in spirit

    b. worship in truth

2. Is there any truth in this chapter on which you want to meditate further, or is there some area of life which you feel the Lord wants you to deal with? In either case, what do you plan to do?

4

Rooting Our Praise in God's Word

PRAISE AND FAITH are popular subjects among Christians in our day. Both are advocated as the solution for all problems large or small, whether they be emotional, physical, or moral, financial or educational, athletic or social. We are told, often in the context of a miraculous experience someone has had, that what you believe is really not important. Simply believe, simply praise, and miracles will occur.

In *Of God and Men*, A.W. Tozer describes the current trendiness of faith:

> Back of this is the nebulous idea that faith is an almighty power flowing through the universe which anyone may plug into at will. . . . When it comes in, out go pessimism, fear, defeat and failure; in come optimism, confidence, personal mastery, and unfailing success in war, love, sports, business and politics. . . .
>
> What is overlooked in all this is that faith is good only when it engages truth; when it is made to rest upon falsehood it can and often does lead to eternal tragedy. For it is not enough that we believe; we must believe the right thing about the right One. . . .

> True faith commits us to obedience. That dreamy, sentimental faith which ignores the judgments of God against us and listens to the affirmations of the soul is deadly as cyanide. . . .
>
> Faith in faith is faith astray.[1]

And praise rooted in such faith is praise astray. It is an outer cosmetic that masks a spiritually bankrupt heart. Not all faith pleases God, nor does all praise.

Praise Rooted in God's Word

God wants us to root our faith and our praise in His Word. He has not given us the Bible as a mere source of inspiration that we can take or leave. In His desire to be personally involved in our lives, He has revealed Himself in written form so that we can understand His attributes, His heart, His values, His plans, His ways. He longs to speak to us through His Word as we take time to listen, to ponder, and to pray. Proverbs 2:1–5 (NIV), says,

> My son, if you accept my words and store up my commands within you, turning your ear to wisdom and applying your heart to understanding, and if you call out for insight and cry aloud for understanding, and if you look for it as for silver and search for it as for hidden treasure, then you will understand the fear of the LORD and find the knowledge of God.

Do we ignore God's Word in our personal lives, yet praise God fervently with other believers? If we do not feed on His Word, our words of appreciation mean little. Imagine how a husband would feel if his wife said, "I love you and enjoy being with you, but please don't talk to me. We'll get along fine as long as you keep quiet." Loving and honoring a person includes valuing his words and taking time for two-way communication.

---

1 A. W. Tozer, *Of God and Men* (Harrisburg, Pa.: Christian Publications, Inc., 1961), 55–57.

Some Christians mentally assent to the inspiration and authority of God's Word, yet fail to learn from it how to live well and how to praise well. In Hebrews 4:12 we read, "The word of God is living and powerful" (NKJV). God's Word can make our praise more dynamic, more life-changing, more pleasing to God.

GOD'S WORD CAN MAKE OUR PRAISE MORE DYNAMIC, MORE LIFE-CHANGING, MORE PLEASING TO GOD.

Psalm 66:2 says, "Make His praise glorious." In order to obey this command, we need not be eloquent, but we must learn to fill our praise with His glories as revealed in His Word. The more we know the Scriptures through prayerful reading, analyzing, and memorizing, the more we will be able to do this.

Praise Filled with God's Word

After Gabriel had announced to Mary that she would bear the Son of the Most High God, she journeyed south by foot or donkey on dusty Palestinian roads to visit her cousin Elizabeth. When she arrived, Elizabeth confirmed the good news that her young cousin would give birth to the Lord.

Mary was deeply moved at how tenderly the Lord had looked upon her and how wondrously He had dealt with her. She offered one of the most magnificent examples of praise recorded:

> My heart is overflowing with praise of my Lord, my soul is full of joy in God my Saviour. For he has deigned to notice me, his humble servant and all generations to come will call me the happiest of women! The One who can do all things has done great things for me—oh, holy is his Name! Truly, his mercy rests on those who fear him in every generation. He has shown the strength of his arm, he has swept away the high and mighty... and lifted up the humble. He has satisfied the hungry with good things and sent the rich away with empty hands. Yes, he has

helped Israel, his child: he has remembered the mercy that he promised to our forefathers (Luke 1:46–55, PHI).

By both paraphrasing and quoting words of inspired praises from many chapters in the Old Testament, Mary filled her praise with rich content from God's Word.

We can learn to do the same, letting the Word of God do its wondrous work in us. Besides the general richness that permeates our praise as we saturate ourselves with God's Word, specific portions can inspire us during our times of praise. The Psalms are filled with praises that we can offer to God, elaborating on them as further thoughts come to mind. Take, for example, Psalm 36:7–9:

> How precious is Thy lovingkindness, O God!
> And the children of men take refuge in the shadow of Thy wings.
> They drink their fill of the abundance of Thy house;
> And Thou dost give them to drink of the river of Thy delights.
> For with Thee is the fountain of life;
> In Thy light we see light.

You can use this for praise just as it is, appreciating what He is to you, to your loved ones who know Him, and to His people everywhere. Sometimes you may want to personalize it and make it less formal:

> How precious is Your lovingkindness, O God! I take refuge in the shadow of Your wings. I drink my fill of the abundance of Your house, And You give me to drink of the river of Your delights. For with You is the fountain of life; in Your light I see light.

At times other translations of the Bible can add freshness to your praise. The last two verses above could be rendered:

I will be satisfied abundantly from Your vast reserves,
And You give me drink from the river of Your delights.
For life's own fountain is within Your presence
And in Your light I am bathed with light.[2]

Psalm 135:3, 5–6 proclaims the Lord's praise to God's people rather than directly to God. You can easily change it into direct worship:

I praise You, Lord, for You are good;
I sing praises to Your name, for it is lovely . . .
I know, Lord, that You are great,
And that You, our Lord, are above all gods.
Whatever You please, You do,
In heaven and in earth, in the seas and in all deeps.

Many portions, such as Psalm 86:5, 10, 12, need no adaptation:

For Thou, Lord, art good, and ready to forgive,
And abundant in lovingkindness to all who call upon Thee . . .
For Thou art great and doest wondrous deeds; Thou alone art God. . . .
I will give thanks to Thee, O Lord my God, with all my heart;
And will glorify Thy name forever.

The New Testament benedictions can also beautify our personal praise. For example, we can use Ephesians 3:20–21 as it is written, or we can paraphrase and personalize it as follows:

I praise You, glorious Father, that by Your power at work within me You are able to do immeasurably more than I can ask or imagine. To You be glory in the Church and in Christ Jesus throughout all generations, forever and ever. Amen.[3]

---

2 *The Old Testament Books of Poetry from Twenty-Six Translations* (Grand Rapids: Zondervan, 1973), 219.

3 "Amen" means, "So let it be," or, "May it be so."

Or we can use Paul's exultant outbursts of praise, such as First Timothy 1:17:

> Now to the King eternal, immortal, invisible, the only God, be honor and glory forever and ever. Amen.

Refocusing Our Hearts

God's Word and praise, working together, speed the growth of our faith and expand our ability to praise. The Holy Spirit uses them to fix our eyes on the Lord. Through them He melts away—as fire melts wax—any resistance to God that has crept into our hearts so that we yield anew to God's supremacy. In true praise we exalt God above our own desires and viewpoints. This helps us pray according to His will and strengthens our confidence that He will answer.

> **IN TRUE PRAISE WE EXALT GOD ABOVE OUR OWN DESIRES AND VIEWPOINTS.**

For some years when I was a widow, my two children and I lived in the castle at Glen Eyrie, The Navigators headquarters in Colorado Springs. We were surrounded by friends and stimulating fellowship. Then in 1966, lured by the advantages of a normal neighborhood, we moved to a home in Pleasant Valley, an eight-minute drive from the Glen.

The morning after we moved, I awoke feeling depressed, isolated, and utterly disinclined to have a quiet time. As I opened my Bible, I told the Lord how I felt. I asked Him to speak to me anyway. My reading that day was Psalm 102, where the writer says, "I am like a pelican in the desert, like an owl moping in the ruin . . . like a lonely bird on the roof" (102:6–7, MNT). As I envisioned these miserable birds, I felt a hint of encouragement. The psalmist had felt even worse than I! Then I joined this godly man as he proceeded to focus on God, who never despises the prayer of the destitute, who hears the groaning of prisoners and sets them free.

God will never change, though everything else may change: location, relationships, surely my feelings. Even the heavens will perish, like a worn-out garment, "But Thou art the same, and Thy years will not come to an end" (Ps. 102:27).

I turned my heart to this unchanging God and praised Him for who He is and always will be, regardless of how my feelings may fluctuate or my faith waver. As I met with God, listened to His Word, and praised Him, He displaced my loneliness with a sense of His unchanging love. He also gave me truths that I could use in praise whenever I was tempted to entertain similar moods.

The Bedouins warn that if you let a camel rest its nose inside your tent, soon it will move its whole body in inch by inch and will take over the entire dwelling. I find that when I give moods of depression half a chance, they behave the same way. But if, through the Word, I turn my thoughts to God and praise Him, He moves the camel out, sometimes quickly, sometimes inch by inch. This happens most readily if I catch the mood when only its nose is in, or at most its head.[4]

Again and again we find that the Lord gives release from dark moods and refreshes our spirit when we use His Word as fuel to kindle our praise. Such praise shifts our attention to God. It disengages our minds from being preoccupied with evils, disappointments, or problems. Beginning with a simple choice to believe God, praise rooted in His Word carries us on to full-fledged faith and cheerful confidence.

4 We are not implying that praise is a quick solution for all depression. Often, especially in severe depression, we must attend to specific causes, including physical ones; and recovery takes time. But even in prolonged depression, focusing on God and praising Him—especially through Scriptures set to music—can rescue from despair and hasten God's healing process.

For Personal Meditation and Group Discussion

1. Why is it important to root both our faith and our praise in God's Word?

2. Which praise portion used in this chapter do you like most? Why?

3. Review the Scriptures used in this chapter and have a time of praise.

5

Blending Praise with Requests

ONE EVENING IN an after-dinner conversation, Henry Wadsworth Longfellow reflected on the discord people would bring into the universe if all their prayers were answered. We mortals would then govern the world rather than God, he mused, and would we govern it better? He decided to avoid this danger by merely giving thanks, silently leaving the rest to God.

Longfellow's indictment of self-willed praying is valid, but his decision only to give thanks and never to make requests is contrary to God's will. Thanksgiving and praise are not substitutes for asking. They are not a superior form of prayer.

Making requests to God is part of His sovereign plan for governing the world and advancing His purposes. He commands us to make requests. He says in Jeremiah 33:3, "Call to Me, and I will answer you"; and in Psalm 50:15, "Call upon Me . . . I will deliver" (KJV).

The call-answer principle held true even for Jesus, to whom God the Father said, "Ask of Me, and I will surely give" (2:8, a prophecy regarding Christ). Jesus in turn said to His disciples, "Ask, using my name, and you will receive, and your cup of joy will overflow" (John 16:24, TLB). Paul wrote to the believers at

Philippi, "In everything . . . let your requests be made known to God" (Phil. 4:6). Asking is part of God's plan.

But in our asking, we are to avoid selfish or childish attitudes. We are not to grasp for control as a frightened passenger might clutch at the steering wheel when danger threatens. God's safeguard against selfish or foolish requesting is not for us to retreat from asking into the safe area of merely giving thanks. Rather it is to know and surrender to the Lord's good, acceptable, and perfect will as revealed in His Word. We are to ask with the basic commitment, "Not my will but Thine be done." E. Stanley Jones said it well: "Prayer is not trying to bend God's will to my will; it is aligning my will to His will."[1]

Our Unprecedented Privilege

Prayer is part of our high calling in Christ. Our Lord Jesus, whom God has exalted as King and High Priest, now shares with us His position of honor. We are sons and daughters of the royal family and priests of the living God—a "royal priesthood," a new kingly order of priests with privileges far exceeding those enjoyed by priests in the Old Testament (1 Pet. 2:9). They burned literal incense on a golden altar in front of a thick, embroidered veil. This veil separated them from God's glorious presence in the holiest part of the Temple. In contrast, the moment we first placed our trust in Christ He qualified us to come boldly into God's holy, majestic presence in prayer.

Whatever our degree of spiritual maturity, our prayers rise to God as a special fragrance. We need not talk to Him in set ways with special rituals. We need not be eloquent. In simple speech we can bring to Him both our personal needs and the needs of others, including their salvation and spiritual growth. We can pray even for impossible things. We need not tell God how or when He should answer; we can just thank Him for what He

1 E. Stanley Jones, *A Song of Ascents* (Nashville: Abingdon, 1968), 104.

is planning to do in His perfect time. If we are not sure what to pray, we can simply say, "Lord, do the things You think best in this situation."

Prayer is a remarkable privilege. Through it we receive benefits that we might otherwise miss, for not all of God's workings on our behalf are automatic. Many of His blessings do come without our asking. He sends His rain even on those who never pray; and often He provides, guides, protects, and strengthens both non-Christians and nonpraying Christians. Yet, in our specific situations, we are not to take for granted that He will provide and protect and enable. It is possible not to have because we fail to ask (James 4:2). We forfeit much if we strive, worry, and manipulate, "eating the bread of anxious toil" as though the Lord were not available to bear the burden of our lives and act on our behalf (Ps. 127:2, RSV).

PRAYER IS A REMARKABLE PRIVILEGE. THROUGH IT WE RECEIVE BENEFITS THAT WE MIGHT OTHERWISE MISS, FOR NOT ALL OF GOD'S WORKINGS ON OUR BEHALF ARE AUTOMATIC.

Through prayer we honor God and experience more of Him. We bring joy to His heart, for "the prayer of the upright is His delight" (Prov. 15:8). Prayer is part of our calling to a personal relationship with the Most High God, possessor of heaven and earth, who longs to see our face and hear our voice (Song 2:14).

Asking and Appreciating

Prayer is the broad term for communicating with God.[2] It includes asking for forgiveness, pouring out our needs before

2 Some people believe that, technically, prayer is only asking. In this book, we present it in its broader, commonly accepted sense.

God, and making requests for ourselves and others. This side of prayer, the *asking* side, is important to God as well as to us, for we are His personal concern. Out of His intensely caring love He wants us to include Him in our experiences and needs, our joys and griefs. He wants us to do this both habitually and in times of crisis. Asking lets God give to us in special ways, and He delights to give.

Prayer also includes praise, thanksgiving, and worship. These form the appreciating side of prayer, in which we give to God. In a manner unique to each of us, we can offer Him the positive responses of our heart. The prayers recorded in the Bible include both appreciation and asking. These biblical prayers would lose much of their vitality and usefulness if we were to delete either their praise or their requests.

The Psalms are a mosaic in which all the components of prayer harmonize like colors in a masterpiece. We do not need unusual creativity to have a prayer life that is beautiful to God, but we do need more than praise, more than requests, more than worship or confession alone. As in the Psalms, every prayer need not contain all the elements of prayer nor need we always use the same order or the same proportion in bringing our requests and our gratitude to God.

But in our overall prayer life, we should include all the components of prayer. The Psalms can teach us to do this. When we read them to God in prayer and expand on the ideas they bring to mind, they give us the feel of how to blend together the appreciating and the asking sides of prayer.

Paul also demonstrates a blend of appreciating and asking. He begins the book of Ephesians with elaborate thanks to God for blessing us with all spiritual blessings, which he lists one after another. Then he asks God to give his readers a clearer realization of their riches in Christ and a vital experience of the entire Trinity (Eph. 1:18–19, 3:14–19). He closes his prayer with worship of "Him who is able to do exceeding abundantly beyond all that we ask or think, according to the power that works within US" (Eph. 3:20).

The Lord commands us to make requests with thanksgiving:

> Don't worry over anything whatever; whenever you pray tell God every detail of your needs in thankful prayer, and the peace of God, which surpasses human understanding, will keep constant guard over your hearts and minds as they rest in Christ Jesus. (Phil. 4:6–7, PHI).

One morning in mid-March, 1984, George and Shirley Osborne, along with six-year-old Alicia, said good-bye to relatives in Omaha.[3] Heading for their home in Newton, Iowa, they approached the ramp onto the interstate highway. Suddenly their Ford Maverick slipped in the snow, skidded across an icy bridge, and went flying through the air, landing upside down. Shirley heard her neck crack. As George helped her out of the car she realized that he was "dragging behind me this thing that was my body."

Shirley's sister wrote us, urgently requesting prayer and describing in detail how much Shirley was suffering. Apart from a miracle, she was likely to remain permanently paralyzed. This weighed on my heart as I (Ruth) went to bed the night we received the letter. I prayed for every need that came to mind and asked for every miracle that would be for the Osbornes' good and the Lord's glory.

Still I lay there anxious, grieved, sleepless. So I began to punctuate my requests with the words, "O give thanks to the Lord, for He is good, for His lovingkindness is everlasting." Over and over I repeated this statement to the Lord, realizing anew why it is the most-used sentence of thankful worship in the Bible. Requests or thanksgiving alone would not have been

3 Before we moved to Singapore, Shirley (then Shirley Atwood) was Warren's secretary.

adequate to relieve my concern. But a combination of asking and thanking helped me pray in faith. It caused God's peace to undergird me and dispel my anxiety. Thankful prayer has likewise upheld Shirley and her loved ones, reinforcing them with God's strength.[4]

Nonjudgmental Praying

Praying with praise and thanksgiving can also help us overcome faultfinding. Even when we pray for others, a critical attitude can easily creep in.

Praying Hyde, a missionary to India, was burdened to pray for an Indian pastor. Thinking of the pastor's coldness and the resulting deadness of his church, Hyde began to pray: "O Father, Thou knowest how cold . . ." Before he could finish the sentence, the words came to mind, "He who touches him, touches the apple of My eye" (Zech. 2:8). Mr. Hyde cried out for God to forgive him for being, like Satan, an accuser of the brethren.

Hyde decided to turn his thoughts from the negatives that were temporarily true in his fellow servant to the things that were both true and lovely. He asked God to show him all that deserved praise in the pastor's life. Much came to mind, and Hyde spent his prayer time thanking and praising God for his Indian brother. Shortly afterwards he learned that, at the very time he was praising and giving thanks, his brother in Christ was greatly revived. Both his life and preaching took on new power.[5]

In the lives of God's children, sin is fleeting. It is not permanent. It is not part of their true nature. In Christ they are cleansed and complete, and God has committed Himself

---

4 You will find the sequel to this story in Chapter 9, "Praising Unconditionally."

5 Francis McGaw, *Praying Hyde* (Minneapolis: Bethany Fellowship, 1970), 52–53.

to finish the good work He has begun in them. We can pray for their spiritual needs, asking God to deliver them, but we must take care to avoid the sin of a judgmental spirit cloaked in prayer.

At one point during our first term in Asia, I (Ruth) found myself filled with a critical attitude toward a spiritual leader. With a subtle sense of superiority, I felt he was simplistic in his teaching on Christian living. He strongly exhorted Christians to obey, but to my knowledge he did not emphasize our enabling through the indwelling Christ.

Then, through the Word, God strongly spoke to me about my proud and critical attitude in judging one of His servants. That was serious. God is the only true Judge, and I was stepping into His shoes. In doing this, I discovered in James 3:14–15, I was aligning myself with the world, the flesh, and the devil. With all my superior knowledge, I myself was failing to abide in Christ. By my pride I was forcing God to oppose me. I was blocking the flow of His grace, for "God opposes the proud but gives grace to the humble" (James 4:6, NIV).

After asking and receiving the Lord's forgiveness, I did some thinking about God's hand of blessing on this Christian brother. God was using him. Could it be that this brother was living according to Romans 6 and 8 and John 15, even though I had not heard him talk about their truths? Admitting to the Lord that I could be wrong about His servant, I prayed, "Lord, I may be mistaken. But if my insight is correct, I ask You to help him. Show him in a new way the simplicity of living by faith in Your indwelling life. Help him to share this with others. And enable me, as well as him, to abide in You constantly."

Months later, when I again heard this man speak, the truths I had been praying about came through clearly in his message. Perhaps I had been right in my insight, and my prayer had helped. Perhaps not. But possibly I would have seen the answer sooner had I been more quick to detect and reject my judgmental attitude. Maybe God's first priority in the situation was to change me, not my brother.

When we pray that God will overcome negatives in another person, we must fortify ourselves against being critical. We can do this by thanking God for the good things in that person, by assuming a humble, I-could-be-wrong attitude, and by praying for our own spiritual needs as well.

Praying with thanksgiving helps us rejoice in the Lord always, even as we pray for others' needs.

Such prayer can promote in our hearts loving attitudes toward other people. Suppose we want to pray for someone who frequently talks about other people's weaknesses and failures. We might say, "Father, I thank You for this brother's zeal and diligence, his heart for You, and his faithful service. Thank You for the ways You have blessed him. Now I may be wrong, but if controlling his tongue is a need in his life, deliver him from gossip and tale-bearing. Keep him—and me—from all misuse of our tongues." Praying for specific negatives should generally be done privately, lest we gossip in prayer.

Praying with thanksgiving helps us rejoice in the Lord always, even as we pray for others' needs. It helps us fix our thoughts on the things that are true, honorable, right, pure, lovely, admirable, morally excellent, and praiseworthy, rather than on their opposites (Phil. 4:8).

Positive, Believing Prayer

Paul's recorded prayers for fellow believers, even those who needed correction, were not centered around negatives. They were centered around thanksgiving and positive goals he had in mind for them. His prayers were progress-centered, not problem-centered. We do well to follow his example.

For the brother who has a way of pointing out other people's failures, we could pray, "Father, thank You that this man is precious and honored in Your eyes. Thank You that You are working in him and using him. I pray that You will give him wisdom when he talks. May his speech honor others, build them up, and impart grace to those who hear him. Thank You for Your mercy toward him and toward me; You do not treat us as our sins deserve. May Your Spirit work in both of us to control our tongues and make us more like Jesus."

If we have repented and received God's forgiveness for known sins in our own life, we can pray in a similar way for our own shortcomings and weaknesses. Positive praying strengthens faith, which assures answers.

We can also stimulate our faith by thanking God in advance for the answer to a prayer. Such thanksgiving goes beyond merely forcing ourselves to mouth a mechanical "thank you." It means viewing the problem from a new viewpoint.

Perhaps we have been weighing our request against inadequate human powers and possibilities. Instead we can visualize a pair of scales and place on one side the contrary facts, the seemingly insurmountable difficulties. On the other side of the scale we can envision God Himself. How great is His power and love? How reliable His promises? We begin to praise Him for who He is, for how vastly He outweighs all difficulties and obstacles. We praise Him for past answers to prayer. Then, out of a heart occupied with who He is, we thank Him for the relative smallness of the difficulties, for the coming answer, and for the ways He will be glorified. Being occupied with Him is the surest way to turn a half-hearted, labored "thank you" into heartfelt thanksgiving.

Thankful prayer does not guarantee favorable circumstances. But it does work wonders in us when we choose it over a disgruntled attitude. Some years ago Ruth and I with our two teenagers were returning from a vacation in Malaysia. Near midnight we were cruising south on a deserted Malaysian highway when I detected the sickening smell of a motor too low on oil. I cannot recall what had happened to the warning light, but our Toyota's engine was ruined. There we sat, stranded on a pitch-black road in an area where robberies were not uncommon. What a blow to my pride as a father and a driver!

What should we do now? We prayed for wisdom and placed ourselves and the Toyota in the Lord's hands. The Lord enabled me to thank Him that He had allowed this, that it would be for our good, and that He was still in control. As I chose to turn my heart to God with thanksgiving, He gave me peace and confidence. He also provided a place to spend the night.

The next day my son, Brian, and I got the car towed to a garage of sorts, which did a good job overhauling the engine.

We experienced various small, immediate blessings from this unplanned expenditure of time and money, but the greatest benefit of praying with thanksgiving was internal: God delivered us from being emotionally and spiritually drained by this stressful situation.

When imprisoned in Philippi, Paul praised the Lord—not because he liked being in jail, but because of how he viewed life (Acts 16). By the Spirit's empowering, Paul made it a practice not to be preoccupied with the things that are seen.

Instead, he constantly turned his attention to the things that are not seen. His perspective in jail included more than the pain of his flogging, the misery of the stocks that bound his feet, and the injustice of it all. It also included the reality of a Savior enthroned above everything in heaven and on earth. It included the power of the resurrected life he shared with Christ, the love of God from which nothing could separate him, and the honor of being counted worthy to suffer for Christ. Instead of filling his thoughts with earthly agonies he filled them with spiritual realities. Therefore he rejoiced and praised.

F.J. Huegel wrote:

> A missionary was passing through a great trial. He had prayed and prayed and prayed, and all to no avail. One day he entered a lonely mission station and found these words in great letters on the front wall: HAVE YOU TRIED PRAISE? He was thunderstruck. It was like the voice of God. He had not tried praise. He would do so at once. Getting down on his knees, he offered hearty praise to God for his great trial and arose refreshed. To his amazement he found not long afterward that all was well. His great problem was solved; the trial was over; his joy was unspeakable. Praise had led to victory.[6]

Growth in Asking and Appreciating

Prayer—both asking and appreciating—is invaluable. It brings answers for ourselves and others. It makes us partners with Christ in accomplishing God's purposes in the world in which He has placed us.

> **Prayer makes us partners with Christ in accomplishing God's purposes in the world in which He has placed us.**

Recording answers to prayer can help us grow in both aspects of praying—in asking and in appreciating. We can review our list of answers often, giving thanks for each reminder of God's goodness and power. This can motivate us to keep bringing our requests to the Lord with thanksgiving.

Another helpful practice is to pray persistently for growth in our prayer life. We can say:

---

6 F.J. Huegel, *Prayer's Deeper Secrets* (Grand Rapids: Zondervan, 1959), 48–49.

> Father, teach me to pray. Teach me to present my requests to You in a setting of thanksgiving and praise. Enable me to occupy my heart with who You are and with what You are doing for me and for others. May I learn to constantly appreciate and adore You. And may I increasingly ask according to Your will as I grow in my knowledge of Your Word.

These requests are according to God's will. Therefore, each time we bring them to God we can add our "Amen" as a forceful statement of trust: "So shall it be."

For Personal Meditation and Group Discussion

1. Why is the asking side of prayer important, both to us and to God?
2. What are some benefits of offering praise and thanksgiving as we make our requests to God?
3. Is there something in this chapter that you want to begin practicing in your prayer life?

6

Praising with Others

CLAUS WESTERMANN, a German scholar, was interned in a prison camp during World War II. He tells about a congregation that learned to praise God during those disastrous years. As they praised together out of deep need, their sorrows and struggles were no longer merely their personal concern, transpiring only between themselves and God. Instead, their trials became "an occurrence in the congregation." Congregational praise fortified them so that they could praise even during enforced isolation from other believers. Westermann wrote:

> Whenever one in his enforced separation praised God in song, or speech, or silence, he was conscious of himself not as an individual but as a member of the congregation. When in hunger and cold, between interrogations, or as one sentenced to death, he was privileged to praise God, he knew that in all his ways he was borne up by the church's praise of God.[1]

Even in normal circumstances we need the strength of public as well as private praise. Each enriches the other. Apart from the fire kindled by corporate worship, we often find it more difficult to maintain warmth and vigor in our personal worship. We need

1 Claus Westermann, *The Praise of God in the Psalms* (Louisville, KY: John Knox Press, 1965), as quoted by Roland Barclay Allen, *Praise! A Matter of Life and Breath* (Nashville: Thomas Nelson Publishers, 1980), 57.

to let the Lord's dynamic presence enfold and nourish us both privately and with others.

In his book on worship, Dr. John MacArthur, Jr., says:

> If believers are to maintain a consistent lifestyle of continuous worship, they need the fellowship and encouragement of other believers as they assemble for group worship. Individual worship and corporate worship feed each other. So on the one hand, I need the fellowship of the saints. On the other hand, the community of saints needs me to live a consistent life of worship.[2]

Biblical Background

In the Old Testament, congregational praise played a prominent role in Israel's relationship with God. Often the people of Israel offered their praise in song, accompanied by harps, by trumpets and flutes, by tambourines and cymbals. Sometimes they included action, clapping their hands or leaping for joy. Sometimes they shouted triumphantly.

As in many Asian countries today, the primary cultural emphasis was on the group rather than the individual. God, of course, has always looked for a personal response of faith in people's hearts, and many of the psalms present personal adoration and appreciation. Yet strictly speaking, in those times praise was vocal expression in company with others more than silent, private adoration.

By both example and teaching, Jesus brought a heightened emphasis on a personal relationship with God, both in worship and in prayer. The Epistles build on this, encouraging a constant personal response of gratefulness to God for His grace and bounty. Yet worshipping with other believers remains an essential, as we read in Colossians 3:16:

---

2 John MacArthur, Jr., *The Ultimate Priority on Worship* (Chicago: Moody Press, 1983), 105.

> Let the word of Christ richly dwell within you, with all wisdom teaching and admonishing one another with psalms and hymns and spiritual songs, singing with thankfulness in your hearts to God.

Effective Corporate Worship

Much of our initial learning to praise takes place in fellowship with others. Enjoying God with people becomes the springboard to greater private enjoyment of Him. A new believer who is involved in good group worship week after week is at a great advantage. Praise is more easily caught than taught.

Each of us can enhance the worship of our church. Or we can dampen it by being distracted and halfhearted, letting our minds wander to the people around us or worrying about the pressures awaiting us. How can we counteract these tendencies and increase our positive influence?

ENJOYING GOD WITH PEOPLE BECOMES THE SPRINGBOARD TO GREATER PRIVATE ENJOYMENT OF HIM.

A few simple ideas can help. On the way to church, pray for the worship service and your part in it. Try to arrive at church a bit early, allowing time to sit quietly and prepare your heart. Pray that you will be attentive to the Lord and that He will give you a fresh experience of praise and worship, along with life-changing insights from His Word. As others enter the sanctuary, pray the same for them.

Then, as the service progresses, purposefully keep turning your heart to God in appreciation, adoration, and readiness to learn. Give special attention to the meaning of the words you sing rather than merely enjoying the nice tunes. Copy for private worship the songs that especially touch your heart.

Ruth and I find that studying the background of hymns helps us sing them with greater understanding and feeling. During my early years as a Christian and my first two terms in Asia, I often studied the life stories of hymn writers and the situations that prompted them to write various hymns. As I realized the joys and sorrows that prompted the writing of the hymns, they came to life in a new way, their meaning intensified.

I marveled at the gifts God gave various hymnists, such as Charles Wesley, who composed 6,000 hymns, and Fanny Crosby, who wrote the lyrics for more than 8,000. For some time Ruth has kept two books on famous hymns in the living room where she can read them when she stops for a coffee break or rests a bit after dinner. You too can heighten your worship experience by learning the stories behind the favorite hymns of your church.

In a worship service, it is not just during the singing or praying or reading of praises from the Bible that God is praised. As in many parts of the Psalms, praise is addressed not only to God but also about God to His people (such as Ps. 34 and 46). This happens as the pastor extols God's character and His works in his message and as individual believers share their insights about God and His goodness to them. No doubt God takes this as praise, even as an architect feels praised if he overhears someone talk about his skills or the beauty of a building he has designed. Whenever we hear God exalted in this way, we can inwardly add praise directly to Him.

As the psalmists praised or made requests, they readily shifted from talking *about* God to talking *to* God (for examples, see Ps. 40, 57, and 73). It seems they did not separate things into strict categories the way we sometimes do. To them, God was personally and directly involved in all of life. So, as they worshipped together, they treated Him as an actual participant in their assembly, as we generally relate to one another in group conversation.

"Dad" Byus was a speaker I (Ruth) especially enjoyed as a student. I remember him as a sprightly old gentleman from the

South, with three little pin curls high on his forehead and the light of God on his face. He spoke with the refreshing simplicity and naturalness of the psalmists.

When Dad Byus extolled and praised the Lord to us in chapel services, he made us thirsty for God as salt creates thirst for water. Then, unannounced, he would break into song to the Lord: "My wonderful Lord, my wonderful Lord, by angels and seraphs in heaven adored."[3] As we sang along with him, we lifted our hearts to our wonderful Lord enshrined at the right hand of the Majesty on high. We sensed more fully what Dad Byus meant when he often quoted another song:

> I have seen the face of Jesus,
> Tell me not of aught beside.
> I have heard the voice of Jesus,
> All my soul is satisfied.[4]

Whether our church worship is spontaneous or formal, we can learn to shift inwardly to praise and thanksgiving in relation to whatever occurs. Vocally or mentally (whichever is most appropriate in our congregation) we can insert our personal "alleluias" and "amens" in thankful exultation and agreement.

Diversity in Worship

A rich diversity exists in the manner of offering worship from person to person, from culture to culture, and from church to church. Some Christians feel worship must always include sound, and some prefer loud sound. Others worship more freely in quietness. Some feel worship and praise must include action. Probably to God these differences do not represent confusion. Each person, each culture, each church offers Him something unique. Each

---

3 Haldor Lillenas, "My Wonderful Lord" (hymn), copyright 1938. 1966 by Lillenas Publishing Co.

4 Frances Bevan, "I Have Seen the Face of Jesus" (hymn), public domain.

person and group can seek to develop an inner excitement about the Lord and find suitable outer expression of this delight.

What if we feel that the worship in our church lacks qualities important to us, such as freshness and spontaneity, or dignity and form? It helps to remember that praise is not a mass function but always the response of individuals to God. Our inner response need not be overly dependent on an atmosphere of excitement or of hushed awe.

REMEMBER THAT PRAISE IS NOT A MASS FUNCTION BUT ALWAYS THE RESPONSE OF INDIVIDUALS TO GOD.

The form of service or the responses of other people need not imprison our praise. We can ask the Lord to enable us to exult in Him even in a congregation where the worship seems cold, uninspiring, and overly structured. Or we can ask Him to help us enjoy a quiet sense of awe and wonder even if the service seems too informal, too devoid of liturgy and structure. We can also pray that God will broaden us so that we can accept and even enjoy greater variety in group praise.

When we are involved in congregational worship, we can enhance our praise by remembering that we worship as part of something larger than our present congregation. We join in the praise of the universal Body of believers of all ages, both present and past.[5]

Various Scriptures also give us glimpses into the Heaven of heavens where God is enthroned in majestic splendor. They portray both the angels and redeemed people responding in joyful assembly with worship and praise (for examples, see Isa. 6 and Rev. 4 and 5). The background music is an unceasing "Holy, holy, holy is the Lord

5 Hebrews 12:22–24 says that we have been allowed to draw near to the city of the living God, the heavenly Jerusalem, with its thousands and thousands of angels in joyful assembly; to the whole church of those enrolled in heaven, and the spirits of righteous men made perfect; to God the Judge of all, and to Jesus, the Mediator of our new covenant, and to His cleansing blood.

God Almighty," and in the foreground we hear glory and honor and thanks to Him who sits on the throne (Rev. 4:8, NIV).

Our heroes and heroines of the faith are in this glorified congregation—Abraham and Sarah, Moses, Deborah, David, John, the apostles, Augustine and his mother Monica, Wesley, William Carey, Hudson Taylor, Adoniram Judson, Henrietta Mears, as well as our loved ones who have preceded us to glory, for they are all "spirits of righteous men made perfect" (Heb. 12:23).

Wherever we are, we can consciously join in the joyful praise of these heavenly worshippers. This does not mean praying to them or trying to communicate with them, but simply delighting in God in company with them.

We can also let our hearts encompass people on earth who are enrolled in heaven. We can include not only those worshipping with us but also other believers in our locality, in our country, in remote parts of the earth. Along with them we worship the King eternal, immortal, invisible, the only God (1 Tim. 1:17).

Realizing that we praise in concert with so vast a choir, we can let our hearts be borne up by the universal love and appreciation that is constantly rising to God. We offer praise with the background music of a cosmic orchestra. We join in the same song of joy that the morning stars sang when God laid the foundations of the earth (Job 38:7). As one hymn says:

> This is my Father's world,
> And to my listening ears
> All nature sings, and 'round me rings
> The music of the spheres.[6]

When we give glory to God, we are joining the response of all creation to God's glorious sovereignty, a response that will reach its fullness when God destroys all discord, ushers in His eternal

---

6 Maltbie D. Babcock, "This Is My Father's World," from *Inspiring Hymns*, compiled by Alfred B. Smith (Grand Rapids: Singspiration, 1951), 286.

Kingdom, and everything in the universe finds its perfection and fulfillment in Christ.

By turning from shallow, halfhearted praise to a wholehearted inner celebration of the Lord, we add blessing to the worship of the entire congregation. Best of all, we bring joy to God who, throughout the world and throughout each group of believers, seeks genuine worshippers.

Thomas Kelly described some unique results of congregational worship—results which we can pray and prepare for in our own worship with other believers:

> A quickening Presence pervades us, breaking down some part of the special privacy and isolation of our individual lives and blending our spirits within a super-individual Life and Power. An objective, dynamic Presence enfolds us all, nourishes our souls, speaks glad, unutterable comfort with us, and quickens us in depths that had before been slumbering.[7]

No wonder David said, "I was glad when they said to me, 'Let us go to the house of the Lord'" (Ps. 122:1).

For Personal Meditation and Group Discussion

1. How can a person make his or her corporate worship more vital?

2. Record several insights from this chapter that could increase heart unity among worshippers of varied preferences in style of worship.

3. Are there ways you plan to make your personal worship with other believers more effective?

---

7 Thomas Kelly, *The Eternal Promise* (Richmond, IN: Friends United Press, 1977), 86, as quoted by Richard J. Foster in *Celebration of Discipline* (San Francisco: Harper and Row, 1978), 143.

7

Making Praise a Lifelong Practice

THE TREND TODAY in personal relationships is most often away from commitments that might involve sacrifice. Many people prefer a nebulous freedom to be themselves. Even in marriage, couples often choose a 50-50 contract to protect each partner's interests rather than vows of self-giving, lifelong love. When couples do make vows, they often view them lightly and break them easily. If we carry over this modern mentality into our relationship with God, we rob ourselves of His full blessing on our lives. We also rob God of the unreserved love and loyal praise for which He yearns.

True worship and praise are highly God-centered activities. They cannot come from an uncommitted, self-centered heart that insists on marching to its own tune rather than to God's. We can offer them only if we have surrendered to Christ as our Lord.

Commitment brings Rewards

What a joy it is to surrender to the Lord! It is like brush and paint surrendering to an artist, or pen and ink to a writer. It is like a violin surrendering to a master violinist or a piano to a concert pianist. In surrendering to the Lord, we submit ourselves to the most creative Person in the universe—the One who can make our lives creative, loving, significant. We were created for Him, and in Him lies our fulfillment. C.H. Spurgeon wrote:

> What the hand is to the lute;
> What the breath is to the flute;
> What the fragrance is to the smell;
> What the spring is to the well;
> What the flower is to the bee
> That is Jesus Christ to me.
> What's the mother to the child;
> What's the guide in pathless wild;
> What is oil to troubled wave;
> What is ransom to the slave;
> What is water to the sea–
> That is Jesus Christ to me.[1]

THE COST OF NONCOMMITMENT FAR EXCEEDS THE COST OF COMMITMENT, FOR SELF-RULE ULTIMATELY BRINGS SELF-RUIN.

In appealing to us for commitment, God offers us what we most want—genuine significance and satisfaction to replace our pursuit of emptiness. He promises special intimacy with Himself, abundant rewards, and the privilege of furthering His eternal purposes in this life and the next. By no means does He guarantee an easy life. But He does promise to spare us the bitter results of going our own way. His way may be harder *for* us, but it is easier *on* us. The cost of noncommitment far exceeds the cost of commitment, for self-rule ultimately brings self-ruin.

Imagine the chaos if the earth were able to rebel against the solar system, stand still in its orbit, and insist that the planets

1 C.H. Spurgeon, in W.Y. Fullerton, *C.H. Spurgeon: A Biography* (London: Williams and Norgate, 1920), 1.

revolve around it rather than around the sun. Such a choice would cause a multitude of problems. It could not succeed because reality is against it.

By submission we put an end to our futile defiance of the basic law of life—that all things be centered in Christ. We plug into reality. In his autobiography, E. Stanley Jones wrote:

> Life is working and working with rhythm and joy. How did it all happen? I asked myself that question as I sat in a hotel room in Alaska writing. I looked up and saw myself in a looking glass and said to myself: "Stanley Jones, you're a very happy man, aren't you?" I replied, "Yes, I am." And then the vital question: "How did you get this way?" And my reply: "I don't know." It is all a surprise to me, a growing surprise. I walked across a field one day, and I stubbed my toe against the edge of a treasure chest, jutting out of the earth. "It's treasure," I cried. Ran off and sold all I had, including myself, and bought that field;[2] and I've been hugging myself ever since that I had sense enough to do it.[3]

Committing Ourselves to God

What gift does God most want from us? God wants us to give Him our whole being. In Romans 12:1 He urges us to give Him our body as a living sacrifice; and in Proverbs 23:26 He says, "Give me your heart, my son, and let your eyes delight in my ways." By a definite act of our will we are to give Him our heart and mind and body, our loyalties, our desires and ambitions, our past, our present, and our future. Surely our commitment to the Lord should be broader and more binding than even the traditional vows of the bride to the bridegroom: the lifelong promise to love, to honor, and to obey.

---

2 This refers to Matthew 13:44, which teaches that a wise person so highly values God's kingdom that he or she gladly forfeits all else in order to possess it.

3 E. Stanley Jones, *A Song of Ascents* (Nashville: Abingdon, 1979), 24.

In our quest for a life of consistent praise, we must be sure we have made this decisive and permanent promise to let Jesus Christ be our only Lord and Master. We must also reaffirm our promise often. Commitment is the heart of worship. Without it our homage is external and unreal.

Though both of us greatly fear careless vows, we have made vows of lifelong commitment to God which we thoughtfully renew from time to time. We do not promise Him something impossible, such as perfect obedience or perfect love. Instead we say, "Lord, I have given You my life, and I want to renew my vows to You. I promise three things: I will seek You, love You, and honor You above all else. I will let You work in me, empowering me as I obey You. I will let You forgive me when I fall into sin, then get up again and continue to walk with You."

Commitment and Praise

King David, a man whose heart attitude God highly commended, often linked praise and thanksgiving with fulfilling one's commitments to the Lord. "Offer to God a sacrifice of thanksgiving," he said, "and pay your vows to the Most High" (Ps. 50:14), "Thy vows are binding upon me, O God; I will render thank offerings to Thee" (56:12), "I will sing praise to Thy name forever, that I may pay my vows day by day" (61:8). The Psalms show David as a man committed to honor God by his life and his praise, and as a man who kept the promises he made to God.

In Psalm 108:1 David said, "O God, my heart is steadfast; I will sing and give praise" (NKJV). Another psalmist wrote, "I will praise the LORD all my life; I will sing praise to my God as long as I live" (146:2, NIV). These men were determined that nothing—no loss, no catastrophe, no circumstance favorable or unfavorable—would deter them from the holy practice of praise. They could not envision a life without praise; the thought would have been unbearable. So they committed themselves to a personal, lifelong celebration of praise to their Creator and King.

If we want praise to penetrate the warp and woof of our being, we need more than pleasant feelings about praise as a nice idea. We need more than pious wishes and fitful starts and stops. A river in Africa heads toward the sea but never gets there. Instead it gets lost in the sands. Our spiritual desires can easily get lost in the sands of secondary interests and marginal activities. Developing a life of praise requires determined commitment, through conscious dependence on the Holy Spirit's work within us. Joseph Carroll wrote:

> No man will ever experience true worship in a consistent manner unless he sets his will to do so. . . . It is not a matter of saying, "I see this truth, and I do want to be a worshiper." No, for we are not what we wish to be or want to be, but what we will to be. You must therefore set your will to become a worshiper of Christ.[4]

To help your soul fulfill its high function of worship and praise, perhaps God would have you, as a definite act of your will, make a commitment to praise Him. As a follow-through, decide how you will begin a consistent practice of praise. You might decide to devote three minutes of your quiet time to praise for several weeks, increasing the time as your capacity grows. Or you could choose to go on an all-praise diet for a week in your prayer life. Or you could make a one-month covenant with your life partner or with a friend, purposing to begin each day, upon arising or at breakfast, with a few minutes of worship, praise, and thanksgiving. Mutual accountability can be a great aid to faithfulness. These appointed times of praise can help prepare you for on-the-spot praise all through the day.

4 Joseph Carroll, *How to Worship Jesus Christ* (Greenville, SC: The Great Commission, Inc., 1984), 13, 32.

To embark on a fresh and lifelong voyage of worship and praise, you might want to start by using a prayer that we have found helpful:

> Lord, I praise You that You are exactly what the Bible says You are—a holy, mighty, and loving God who does wonderful things for those who trust You. I commit myself to seek Your face regularly, to do Your will, and to submissively let You work within me, giving me both the will and the power to obey You in all things, including praise and worship. May the living reality of who You are motivate me every day in new ways to a continuous lifestyle of praise. May I know You better day by day. May my earnest praise be the glad overflow of a heart that trusts and exults in You. "O God, my heart is steadfast; I will sing and give praise."

For Personal Meditation and Group Discussion

1. List several reasons why it makes sense to surrender to Christ as our Lord.

2. Have you given your life unreservedly to Christ? If not, list the things that are hindering you. What would the Lord have you do about them?

3. Write down several ways you could assure a more consistent practice of praise, and select one for your immediate use.

Part II

Questions

Is praise a cure for every ailment, a guarantee that life will run smoothly? Is God a heavenly vending machine into which we insert the coin of praise, press the right button, and get whatever we want? Does God intend that we give thanks for everything that happens, the evil along with the good?

The following chapters seek to answer questions that can keep us from worship or rob us of its joys.

8

Worshipping, Praising, and Giving Thanks

PROBLEMS ARISE WHEN family members take one another for granted or withdraw from close relating. A mother cooks, cleans, and provides special treats, yet her teenagers scarcely notice she exists. A husband submerges himself in his career while his wife yearns (and maybe nags) for a closer relationship. An adolescent treats her adoring young brother as though he were nothing, withholding even crumbs of positive attention unless she wants him to do her a favor.

Relationships deepen when we treat one another with affection and appreciation. They deteriorate when we ignore loved ones or use them as means to our own ends, with little or no thought about their needs. Many people can identify with the despairing young woman who recently revealed her greatest heartache: "He treated me like a nonperson."

God has created us in His image as personal, relationship-oriented beings. Our desires for closeness with friends and loved ones reflect similar longings in God's heart, though often we distort the reflection by our self-centeredness. Like us, God is a Person with feelings and desires, and His desires center in loving relationships. Unlike us, He is not threatened when we take

Him for granted or seek Him only for our own ends. He does not withdraw or lose His temper. But He is grieved, because He yearns for vital intimacy with us, intimacy that can fill our emptiness and satisfy His longings.

When we express our love to the Lord, we help to complete His enjoyment of being our Father, much as a small daughter's hugs and kisses heighten her daddy's enjoyment of fatherhood, or a wife's admiration enhances her husband's delight in marriage. God receives genuine pleasure as we praise and worship Him.

In this chapter we seek to clarify what worship, praise, and thanksgiving are and how they relate to one another. More important, we give examples of how people in the Scriptures worshipped, praised, and gave thanks. By meditating on the passages from God's Word you will gain a more vivid sense of what these terms mean.

> **God receives genuine pleasure as we praise and worship Him.**

Worship the King

The usual words for *worship* in the original languages of the Bible, Hebrew and Greek, mean "to bow down" in awe or homage, much as people throughout the ages have bowed before earthly monarchs. We read in Psalm 95:6–7:

> Come, let us worship and bow down;
> Let us kneel before the Lord our Maker.
> For He is our God.

Our English word *worship* comes from an old Anglo-Saxon word that we today would spell "worthship." It basically means to ascribe worth to a person or object. In relation to God, it means to regard Him with the deepest respect and adoration, to attribute supreme value to Him, or to pay honor to Him by an act of reverence.

Rather than offering us a precise definition of worship, the Bible provides a motivating, often exhilarating, sense of what it is. Throughout the Scriptures people expressed their worship in several ways. They bowed before God as an act of homage or awed wonder. They ascribed glory to Him through praise and thanksgiving. They offered special gifts to Him, the chief gift being the consecration of themselves to be wholly His. They honored Him through temple worship with its ceremonies and sacrifices.

So we might define worship as bowing our hearts before the Lord with sincere reverence and devotion, giving Him our admiration, our appreciation, and ourselves. Often the word *worship* is used to denote the whole of our positive, grateful, adoring response to God, whether private or public, silent or spoken. Worship might be called the crown in which the jewels of praise and thanksgiving are mounted.

Praise and Thanksgiving

These jewels that beautify the crown of worship are similar to each other, yet different. We see this in the prayers recorded in the Old Testament, where in English *praise* and *thanksgiving* honor God in distinctive ways, but with considerable overlap. *Thanksgiving* reveals gratitude for God's nurturing qualities and His constant acts of care. *Praise* at times shows appreciation for these same things, but it also expresses admiration—often jubilant admiration—for God's strong qualities and His mighty works as the sovereign Creator who controls and sustains the entire cosmos.

In the New Testament both thanksgiving and praise generally express appreciation for what God does. But we also find delightful examples of praise for who God is—for His incomparable greatness and His worthiness to receive glory forever and ever. When we show appreciation in ordinary life today, we come close to the way the words *thanksgiving* and *praise* are used in the Bible. We thank people largely out of gratefulness for what they do—for services and gifts. Yet occasionally we say, "Thank you for being so loving and thoughtful," or even, "Thank you for being you!" We praise people out of admiration for what they do (their achievements as well as their good deeds) and for who they are (their character, abilities, appearance, and position). So, praise and thanksgiving show appreciation both for what people do and what they are, but in somewhat different ways. For an easy-to-remember description we could say that *thanking shows gratefulness; praise shows admiration.*

In the prophetic vision God gave in Revelation 7, the Apostle John witnessed in heaven a dramatic blending of worship, praise, and thanksgiving. Before the throne of God and the Lamb he saw a vast, innumerable multitude from every nation, tribe, people, and language. Robed in white, they were honoring God with loud voices. All the angels, who stood encircling the throne, prostrated themselves before it and worshipped God, saying:

> Amen!
> Praise and glory
> and wisdom and thanks and honor
> and power and strength
> be to our God for ever and ever.
> Amen! (Rev. 7:12, NIV)

In this preview of the future, the angels provide an excellent model as they worship the Lord with exultant praise and thanksgiving.

Praise His Excellent Greatness

The hallmark of praise is admiration for the perfection and greatness of God and for His mighty works. This admiration takes a number of forms and expresses a variety of emotions.

Many Hebrew words in the Old Testament are translated by the word *praise* or by similar words that enlarge our sense of what praise includes. Some of these words mean to laud or boast, to celebrate, to sing, to shout for joy, to exclaim, to proclaim a high opinion of the Lord, and to bless Him.[1] Still other words mean to exalt the Lord, to exult in Him, to extol Him, or to magnify, glorify, and honor Him.

BECAUSE GOD LOOKS ON OUR HEART AND KNOWS ALL OUR THOUGHTS, WE CAN ALSO EXPRESS OUR ADMIRATION AND DEVOTION SILENTLY.

These words for *praise* in Hebrew are words involving sound (either speech or music) and sometimes action, such as kneeling, lifting one's hands, or plucking the strings of an instrument. Many people, even in their times alone with God, experience greater concentration and enjoyment if they praise and give thanks vocally, or at least in a whisper. Because God looks on our heart and knows all our thoughts, we can also express our admiration and devotion silently. This allows us to respond to Him on many occasions when speaking or singing aloud would be unacceptable.

A variety of Greek words in the New Testament are also translated by the word *praise* and related words. They carry the thought of praising, glorifying, blessing, eulogizing, holding in high honor, extolling, declaring the excellencies of, singing hymns to, exulting in, boasting of, and being glad in the Lord.

These words from the Old and New Testaments reveal different facets of praise. Thinking about them one by one and using them as we magnify the Lord can make our praise more rich and gratifying.

---

1 When we bless God, we express appreciation to God, acknowledging Him to be the source of blessings and benefits in our lives, as in Psalm 103: 1–5. The NIV uses *praise* where the NASB, KJV, and others use *bless*.

Besides offering praise with our lips, we are to "be to the praise of His glory," causing praise by our lives (Eph. 1:6). When we are filled with the fruits of righteousness and let our light shine by doing good works, the result is glory and praise to God by people who observe our lives.

The Scriptures abound with motivating examples of praise. Often these passages of praise show admiration for God's majesty, His supremacy, His power, and His spectacular acts in the world at large and in the universe.

Nebuchadnezzar, absolute ruler of the mightiest empire of his time, learned through crushing humiliation that only God is all-powerful. As he told what had happened to him, he expressed his newborn awe of God in a beautiful example of praising God's greatness:

> I Nebuchadnezzar, raised my eyes toward heaven . . . and I blessed the Most High and praised and honored Him who lives forever;
>
> For His dominion is an eternal dominion,
> And His kingdom endures from generation to generation.
> And all the inhabitants of the earth are accounted as nothing,
> But He does according to His will in the host of heaven
> And among the inhabitants of earth;
> And no one can ward off His hand
> Or say to Him: "What hast Thou done?" . . .
>
> Now I Nebuchadnezzar praise, exalt, and honor the King of heaven, for all His works are true and His ways just, and He is able to humble those who walk in pride. (Dan. 4:34–35, 37).

Psalm 150 climaxes the psalms with a call for resounding praise. Verse 2 says: "Praise Him for His mighty deeds, praise Him according to His excellent greatness." We are to praise God both for the great things He does and for the glorious person He is.

Give Thanks, for He is Good

As we have noted earlier, thanksgiving basically reveals gratitude for God's nurturing qualities and for His works in caring for us. Psalm 107:8 provides a good example of giving thanks for both who God is and what He does: "Let them give thanks to the LORD for his unfailing love and his wonderful deeds for men" (Ps.107:8).

Often the psalmists offered thanks for God's goodness, lovingkindness, and faithfulness—for the loving and merciful side of His nature, for His unwavering intent to bless and protect those who trust Him. These nurturing attributes reveal the heart from which His loving actions flow. The Bible is filled with passages that can stimulate us to thank God for who He is. For example:

> The LORD's lovingkindnesses indeed never cease,
> For His compassions never fail.
> They are new every morning;
> Great is Thy faithfulness. (Lam. 3:22–23)

Those of us who reverence the Lord will never lack any good thing (Ps. 34:10, TLB).

> Do not fear, for I am with you;
> Do not anxiously look about you, for I am your God.
> I will strengthen you, surely I will help you,
> Surely I will uphold you with My righteous right hand.
> (Isa. 41:10)

God is utterly reliable. His love is unfailing, His promises irreversible. He has obligated Himself to meet our needs as His trusting servants, putting Himself under bonds of commitment. We see this in Isaiah 41:10, quoted above, where He confirms and reconfirms His intentions: "I will . . . surely I will . . . surely I will." He will never fail to take care of us. He will never let us down. No wonder Israel's favorite statement of appreciation to

God was, "Oh give thanks to the LORD, for He is good, / For His lovingkindness is everlasting" (Ps. 107:1).

Besides giving thanks for who the Lord is, Old Testament worshippers constantly thank Him for what He does. Their thanks rise to Him for both routine and special acts of care:

> What shall I render to the LORD
> For all His benefits toward me?
> . . . .
> I shall offer a sacrifice of thanksgiving,
> And call upon the name of the LORD. (Ps. 116:12, 17).

Thanksgiving is even more prominent in the New Testament than in the Old. People give thanks for God's acts of mercy and His material provisions. We also see frequent examples of thanksgiving for fellow believers. Paul was continually giving thanks for the people he had led to Christ. He wrote, "I thank my God in all my remembrance of you, always offering prayer with joy in my every prayer for you all" (Phil. 1:3–4). But most of all he encouraged thanksgiving for our lavish spiritual blessings and for God's gracious working in our lives. He wrote, "Thanks be to God, who always leads us in His triumph in Christ" (2 Cor. 2:14). And he prayed that the Colossian believers would give joyful thanks to the Father, "who has qualified us to share in the inheritance of the saints in light" (Col. 1:12).

Blending Worship, Praise, and Thanksgiving

Often praise and thanksgiving are blended together in the Psalms like colors in a painting. Psalm 57 is a superb example. David composed this psalm while hiding in a cave when he fled from Saul. He cried out to God for deliverance and expressed confidence that it would come. Then he sang,

> Awake, my soul!
> Awake, O harp and lyre!

> I will awake the dawn!
> I will *give thanks to thee*, O Lord, among the peoples;
> I will *sing praises to thee* among the nations.
> For thy steadfast love is great to the heavens, thy faithfulness to the clouds.
> Be exalted, O God, above the heavens! Let thy glory be over all the earth! (Ps. 57:8–11, RSV).

Psalm 111 also offers a delightful blend of praise and thanks to God for both His majestic greatness and His compassionate care for His people. Here are some excerpts:

> Praise the LORD!
> I will give thanks to the LORD with all my heart.
> . . . .
>
> Splendid and majestic is His work . . .
> The Lord is gracious and compassionate . . .
> He has given food to those who fear Him
> . . . .
>
> Holy and awesome is His name . . . His praise endures forever (111:1, 3–5, 9–10).

Various passages of Scripture also link worship with praise or thanksgiving. Psalm 99 begins by turning our attention to the Lord's supremacy: "The LORD reigns . . . He is enthroned . . . The Lord is great . . . and He is exalted above all the peoples." Then the psalm encourages us to praise and worship this God of majestic holiness:

> Let them *praise* Thy great and awesome name;
> Holy is He.
> . . . .
>
> Exalt the LORD our God,
> And *worship* at His holy hill;
> For holy is the LORD our God. (99:3, 9)

Second Chronicles 29:30 also connects praise and worship: "So they sang praises with joy, and bowed down and worshiped." In Revelation 11:16–17, the elders combined thanksgiving and worship as they

> Fell on their faces and worshiped God, saying, "We give Thee thanks, O Lord God, the Almighty, who art and who wast, because Thou hast taken Thy great power and hast begun to reign."

More Important than Definition

God has put within us a profound need to admire and adore someone unreservedly, with no danger of being disappointed. He meets this need as we worship and praise Him for His infinite perfections and His awe-inspiring works. As we learn to open the sluice gates of our heart and pour out to Him our delighted esteem, He releases and expands our spirit to experience more of Him. We minister to Him through worship, praise, and thanksgiving. He in turn ministers to our deep inner needs.

> **GOD HAS PUT WITHIN US A PROFOUND NEED TO ADMIRE AND ADORE SOMEONE UNRESERVEDLY, WITH NO DANGER OF BEING DISAPPOINTED.**

For years we have found First Chronicles 29:11–15 a greatly motivating passage for worship, praise, and thanksgiving. This passage blends together these three aspects of appreciative prayer.

The people of Israel had willingly brought lavish gifts for building the Temple of the Lord. King David was deeply thankful. His great dream was beginning to come true—his dream that the greatest of kings should have a home worthy of His excellency. So David blessed the Lord his God in the presence of all the assembly, saying:

> Thine, O Lord, is the greatness and the power and the glory and the victory and the majesty, indeed eveything that is in the heavens and the earth; Thine is the dominion, O Lord, and Thou dost exalt Thyself as head over all.
>
> Both riches and honor come from Thee, and Thou dost rule over all, and in Thy hand is power and might; and it lies in Thy hand to make great, and to strengthen everyone. (1 Chron. 29:11–12)

After this exultant outpouring of adoration David said, "Therefore, our God, we *thank* Thee, and *praise* Thy glorious name" (29:13). When he had finished his prayer, the people worshipped: "All the assembly blessed the Lord . . . and *bowed low and did homage* to the Lord" (29:20).

Passages like this give us living demonstrations of worship, praise, and thanksgiving. They mingle together gratitude, admiration, exultation, and adoration in ways that defy strict distinctions. For many of us—perhaps all of us—such models help us glorify the Lord more than definitions do. Defining the terms we use can enrich our worship.[2] But more important than defining is actually offering God our love, our admiration, and our gratitude.

Worship, praise, and thanksgiving are highly significant ways of relating to God. Through this delightful trio of responses we can deepen our fellowship with Him and meet longings in His heart. Therefore let us worship Him, praise Him, and give thanks to Him, silently and vocally, alone and with others, with or without precise definitions. Let us express to God our deep appreciation for what He is and for what He does. He is worthy.

---

2 The introduction gives further thoughts on the meanings of worship, praise, and thanksgiving.

For Personal Meditation and Group Discussion

1. Why are worship, praise, and thanksgiving important to God?
2. Mark the statements in this chapter that you most want to remember.
3. Review the chapter again, especially the Scriptures used, and have a time of worship, praise, and thanksgiving.

9

Praising Unconditionally

WHY DO WE PRAISE GOD? Do we desire to honor Him and make Him glad? Or do we feel that praise puts God under obligation to grant the earthly longings we bring to Him in prayer? Will God do whatever we ask simply because we praise Him?

God is not a heavenly vending machine into which we insert the coin of praise, press the right button, and get whatever we want. Nor is praise a magical incantation that forces God to fulfill our wishes. Many of us would not consciously try to manipulate God. But when we praise Him in the midst of a trial, we can be tempted to secretly bargain with Him, feeling in some recess of our heart, "I'm praising You, Lord. Now You owe it to me to work out this situation the way I want."

Trusting Regardless of What Happens

True praise imposes no conditions on God. It chooses to believe Him regardless of the situation and its outcome. It accepts the circumstances He has permitted, without insisting that He change them. Such praise begins with the attitude that says, "Father, I'm going to keep trusting You even though everything is dark and confusing." As we continue to praise, we reach the place where we can say, "Father, thank You that You are working in me to beautify my character. Don't remove this problem until You've done all You want to do through it, in me and in others. Use it to prepare me for the future You have in mind for me. Change me in any way You see fit."

One major purpose of trials is to strengthen our faith and transform our attitudes. Therefore, choosing an attitude of trust and praise sometimes ends a trial with surprising speed. But even if it does not, we find ourselves enriched and strengthened to endure.

ONE MAJOR PURPOSE OF TRIALS IS TO STRENGTHEN OUR FAITH AND TRANSFORM OUR ATTITUDES.

Since the morning of her accident in early 1984, Shirley Osborne has learned in new ways to offer unconditional praise.[1] After days of excruciating pain and months of rehabilitation, she remained largely paralyzed from her shoulders down, apart from some movement in her arms. Friends and relatives helped George remodel their home to accommodate her wheelchair, and a few months later she moved home.

From the first, Shirley gave thanks in this trial, not because she felt thankful but because she chose to obey her sovereign, all-wise God. She and George have submitted to God as their Potter, desiring that "the bottom line be God's glory."

Recently we received a cassette in which Shirley testifies to God's faithfulness and affirms her unconditional faith. Although it appears that no more natural healing can be expected, friends assure her that they are asking God to restore the full use of her body. Shirley says, "And I believe God for complete healing, too. I really do. But we must remember that our faith is in God's trustworthiness." With or without further healing, she is trusting God's faithfulness.

1 The details of Shirley's accident are in Chapter 5.

Daniel 3 has deeply influenced George and Shirley. It tells the story of Shadrach, Meshach, and Abednego, who refused to bow to the golden image of King Nebuchadnezzar. Hoping to dissuade them of their folly, the king said in a rage, "What god is there who can deliver you out of my hands?" (Dan. 3:15). They replied, "*Our God* whom we serve *is able to deliver us* from the furnace of blazing fire; *and He will deliver us* out of your hand, O king. *But even if He does not*, let it be known to you, O king, that we are not going to serve your gods or worship the golden image that you have set up" (3:17–18). Infuriated, the king had the three young men cast into the blazing furnace.

Their miraculous deliverance has inspired faith down through the centuries. As Shirley prays for a miracle, she echoes the confidence of these men in Daniel 3: "My God is able, and He will deliver me. But if He doesn't, I won't turn from Him. 'Though He slay me, yet will I trust in Him'" (Job 13:15). Through the grace of God, she trusts not only God's ability but also His wisdom.

Shirley's life is filled with reasons to be incessantly disgruntled, and at times she fails when her attitudes are tested. But she continues to follow Christ in His basic commitment to the Father: "Not My will, but Thine be done" (Luke 22:42). She submits her desires to God and offers unconditional praise.

Demonstrating Our Trust

Through praise each of us can demonstrate trust in God to work in the present as He has in past centuries. In the final chapters of Genesis we see how God brought far-reaching benefits through all the events that had happened to Joseph—the cruel betrayal by his brothers, the agonies of his soul, the slavery, the false accusations, the long years of imprisonment, and the forgetfulness of the butler he had befriended, with the extra years of confinement that resulted.

We read in Psalm 105 that God Himself had sent Joseph to Egypt, intending to bring good out of his trials (Ps. 105:17). He used them to prepare this youth to be prime minister of the greatest nation on earth. Through Joseph's trials, God arranged to have him in the right place at the right time to save the lives of hundreds of thousands during a severe famine. Joseph's long years of suffering resulted in his own life being saved, as well as his entire family, and through it, the ancestors of Jesus.

Joseph showed his confidence in God's loving sovereignty in Genesis 50. When his brothers feared retribution, Joseph told them, "You meant evil against me, but God meant it for good in order to bring about this present result, to preserve many people alive. So therefore, do not be afraid" (Gen. 50:20–21). As we offer praise, we show that we believe that Joseph's God is alive and at work today, even in the bleakest of circumstances.

Through praise we follow the example of Paul and Silas in their painful imprisonment at Philippi. There in the inner prison, with their feet fastened in stocks, they were praying and singing at midnight. Suddenly God miraculously released them through an earthquake (Acts 16). Or we emulate Paul when he later rejoiced in the Lord though imprisoned for years. He was confident that his suffering was accomplishing God's purposes and therefore his own deepest desires.

Releasing the Transforming Power of Christ

God does not promise to make our troubles vanish and our wishes come true if we praise Him. But in the twentieth century as in the first, praise often releases the transforming power of Christ in both our characters and our situations.

A woman who had struggled for years as the wife of an alcoholic finally divorced him. Later she came into a fresh, vital walk with God and learned the importance of praise and thanksgiving. She began to thank God for her ex-husband, for allowing his alcoholism, and for the years of heartache she had experienced. As she continued to praise, she became aware of her own self-righteous, superior attitude toward him. She saw how she had immersed herself in joyless self-pity and martyrdom. So she confessed her sin, acknowledging that her pride was worse than her husband's alcoholism. Then she continued to praise and rejoice.

As time went by, her ex-husband, miles away with no direct influence from her, trusted Christ and found deliverance from drinking. In time he returned to her, and they began a new life together. Through praise, mingled with submission to the Lord, this woman prepared the way for God to remove the log from her eye and the splinter from her husband's.

When Fanny Crosby was six weeks old, she lost her sight because a doctor applied the wrong medicine to her eyes. What a valid reason to go through life bitter and useless! But Miss Crosby developed into a woman of outstanding faith and praise. She wrote more than 8,000 hymn poems, many of which are still popular today. Among them is this familiar song:

> All the way my Savior leads me
> What have I to ask beside?
> Can I doubt His tender mercy,
> Who through life has been my guide?
> Heavenly peace, divinest comfort,
> Here by faith in Him to dwell!
> For I know, whate'er befall me,
> Jesus doeth all things well.[2]

This gifted woman also penned the invigorating words of "To God Be the Glory" and "Blessed Assurance." Would she have written with the same insight and power had she not been blind? We cannot be sure. But she felt she could not have written thousands of hymns had she been distracted by seeing all the

---

2 Fanny Crosby, "All the Way My Savior Leads Me," from *Inspiring Hymns*, compiled by Alfred B. Smith (Grand Rapids: Singspiration, 1951), 22.

interesting and beautiful objects in the world around her. In her autobiography she wrote, "It seemed intended by the Blessed Providence of God that I should be blind all my life, and I thank Him for the dispensation."[3] Her positive, God-centered, thankful attitude transformed tragedy into triumph. By it she, though dead, still speaks to us.

A Major Stress Reducer

Praise and thanksgiving do not insulate us from problems and pressures. But as we couple them with honest prayer, they do serve as a major stress reducer. They help release us from the self-imposed stresses of our negative attitudes, opening our hearts to the soothing power of God's peace, which surpasses all understanding. And they do more than soothe. They also infuse us with vitality. God's Word says, "Strength and joy are in His place" (1 Chron. 16:27); and "The joy of the LORD is your strength" (Neh. 8:10).

> **PRAISE AND THANKSGIVING DO NOT INSULATE US FROM PROBLEMS AND PRESSURES. BUT AS WE COUPLE THEM WITH HONEST PRAYER, THEY DO SERVE AS A MAJOR STRESS REDUCER.**

Praise and thanksgiving usher us into God's presence, where we can partake of His joy and quietly absorb strength, strength for our every need—spiritual, emotional, or physical. Through moments of praise we can brighten each day with dozens of mini-vacations that restore our soul. At each point of need, regardless of external pressures, we can learn to enjoy an inner pause that refreshes.

3 *Fanny Crosby's Life Story* (New York, 1903), quoted by Warren W. Wiersbe in "Fanny Crosby—Blind to See God," *Good News Broadcaster*, April 1982, 30.

By helping us view our situation through God-colored glasses, praise gives our threatening or depressing circumstances a new look. It helps us relax our bungling efforts to change other people so that life will be easier for us. It tunes us in to God's wisdom so that we know when to take wise, loving action and when to simply trust Him to act. We begin to exert a creative, uplifting influence on others, because as we change, people tend to react to us in new ways. Although God does not promise fewer trials if we praise, praise often brings a multitude of external benefits as well as a relaxed-yet-invigorated spirit.

Our unconditional praise deepens our trust and joy in God. It increases our spiritual impact on people. These and other benefits come not as our due for praising the Lord but simply as added reasons to praise Him for His undeserved favor. They come not because we manipulate God to do what we want, but because we center our thoughts and expectations in Him.

Our motive in genuine praise is to bring joy and glory to God. We are here to do His will, not to obligate Him to do ours.

For Personal Meditation and Group Discussion

1. Review the benefits of praise mentioned throughout this chapter and record the ones that most impress you.

2. How and in what situations might we misuse praise?

3. Choose some difficult situation that you or someone dear to you is facing, and begin to offer unconditional praise as you pray about it.

10

Giving Thanks Always

GOD HAS PLANTED within us a quiet, supernatural agent of change. This secret agent is the Holy Spirit. He has been sent from the headquarters of the universe to live in us and glorify God through us here in enemy territory. In fulfilling His mission, one of His basic strategies is to stage an ongoing revolution in the way we look at life.

Using the Word of God, He seeks to overcome our short-sighted, distorted viewpoints by teaching us to see things from God's perspective. This means looking beyond the apparent to the real. It means looking beyond life's joys, beyond life's difficulties and struggles, to God's glorious purposes for both the present and the future.

This change of viewpoint prepares us for one of the profound differences the Holy Spirit makes in our lives: the ability to give thanks constantly in the varied circumstances of life. Ephesians 5:20 speaks of "giving thanks always for all things to God the Father in the name of our Lord Jesus Christ" (NKJV). Two verses earlier Paul charges us to let the Holy Spirit fill us. As we cooperate with the Spirit and trust Him to work in us, He enables us to adopt a radically transformed attitude toward all things. By natural bent, many of us tend to take the credit for the good that comes our way and blame someone else—even

God—for the bad. Through thanksgiving the Holy Spirit enables us to trust God's good purposes even when things seem to go wrong.

Another verse that emphasizes habitual thanksgiving is First Thessalonians 5:18: "In everything give thanks, for this is God's will for you in Christ Jesus." In a similar vein, Hebrews 13:15 encourages us to "continually offer up a sacrifice of praise to God." Notice the theme of constancy that runs through these verses: "always . . . in everything . . . continually." Our Lord desires a continuous flow of thanksgiving and praise from us as His children. He wants to produce in us a spiritual aptitude for giving thanks at all times, in all situations, for all things.

THROUGH THANKSGIVING THE HOLY SPIRIT ENABLES US TO TRUST GOD'S GOOD PURPOSES EVEN WHEN THINGS SEEM TO GO WRONG.

For All Things Without Exception?

"In everything give thanks"—this is neither natural nor easy. "Giving thanks always for all things" sounds even more difficult and, to some thoughtful people, inappropriate or even absurd. They object, "How can I possibly give thanks for stubbing my toe, going bankrupt, or losing a loved one? Or for injustice, terrorism, war? It doesn't make sense."

Sincere students of Scripture differ as to what Paul had in mind when he wrote "giving thanks always *for all things*." Some believe that it means thanking God for all His benefits to us, both physical and spiritual, both past and present. They feel it also includes thanks for future blessings: for the assured fulfillment of His promises to those who trust Him, for anticipated answers to prayer, and for the magnificent future He has planned for us and for the whole cosmos. They base their conclusion on the context of the verse and on biblical examples of thanksgiving, including Paul's own prayers.

Kenneth Wuest is among the men of knowledge who hold this view. He quotes *Expositor's Greek New Testament* as saying,

> The "for all things" is taken by many in its widest possible extent as including things evil as well as good. The Epistle does not deal, however, particularly with the *sufferings* of the Christian, but with what he receives from God and what his consequent duty is. It is most accordant therefore with the context to understand the 'all' as referring to all the *blessings* of the Christian, the whole good that comes to him from God.[1]

Others believe that Paul intended "all things" to be all-inclusive, covering everything that happens in our lives and in the world. Foremost in their thinking is our response to trials. They view distressing or evil events as blessings in disguise. They also vouch for the benefits they reap from literally thanking God even for distressing or evil events. They find that giving thanks for their specific trials brings a deeper alignment with God than merely thanking Him for obvious blessings.

The Wycliffe Bible Commentary supports this all-inclusive position. It says,

> *Giving thanks always.* No limit on the time . . . *For all things.* No limit on the extent. Some would restrict this to the blessings mentioned in the epistle, but it seems better to take it in its widest sense (see Romans 8:28).[2]

William Barclay also joins the expositors who hold this second view. He speaks of Chrysostom, the great preacher of the fourth century, who felt that a Christian could even give thanks

1 Quoted by Kenneth Wuest in *Ephesians and Colossians in the Greek New Testament* (Grands Rapids: Eerdmans, 1957), 128.

2 Alfred Martin, *The Wycliffe Bible Commentary*, Everett F. Harrison, ed. (Chicago: Moody Press, 1962), 1314.

for hell, which is a warning that prods people to choose the right way. Barclay gives reasons why the early church was a thankful church:

> Its members were still dazzled with the wonder that God's love had stooped to save them . . . never had men such a consciousness that they were in the hands of God. They were able to give thanks for all things, because they were convinced that all things came from God.[3]

Even after prayerful, open-minded consideration of this issue, we will not all agree in our conclusions. Some will believe that God asks us to give thanks *for* all circumstances. Others will be convinced that we are to give thanks *in* all circumstances for all His benefits to us. In issues like this we should avoid pressing others to have identical convictions or judging the validity of their thanksgiving. Instead, whatever our view, God wants us to act on the light we have received.

In our own lives we often thank God for distresses and trials. Yet at other times we reap equal benefits from thanking Him during trials for who He is and how He is going to use them for good as we trust Him. We also find that it helps our hearts tremendously to thank Him for all the resources we have in Christ and for our exalted position in Him, which is unaffected even by the worst of circumstances.

Whichever form our thanksgiving takes, God uses it to lift us from being under the load of our situation to being on top of it. Giving thanks prepares us to cooperate with Him rather than resist Him, to rejoice rather than complain.

As we give thanks, God looks beyond our actual words to our heart response. He looks for a trusting attitude that enjoys His blessings, receives His more than sufficient grace, and accepts trials as instruments that He will use for good.

---

3 William Barclay, *Letters to Galatians and Ephesians* (Edinburgh: The Saint Andrew Press, 1954), 197–198.

Trusting Our Sovereign God

To thank God continually, whatever happens, is nonsense from the human point of view. But God's Word gives us another viewpoint based on the loving sovereignty of God. Romans 8:28 says, "God causes all things to work together for good to those who love God, to those who are called according to His purpose." Here, in the context of Romans 7 and 8, "all things" includes adversity, pain, disappointment, and even failure. And the good that results includes becoming more like God's Son—the best thing that could happen to *us* (Rom. 8:29).

If we rely on our feelings, our short-term perspective, or our shallow understanding, we will not be able to give thanks regardless of what happens. We must learn to choose God's viewpoint and to believe what He promises to do.

> **GOD OVERSEES THE EVENTS THAT INFLUENCE MY LIFE—EVEN THE HAPPENINGS AND CONTACTS THAT SEEM TO OCCUR BY CHANCE.**

Several years ago Ruth and I saw the following quotation in a home in India: "God is the Blessed Controller of all things." This is Phillips' rendering of "the blessed and only sovereign" in First Timothy 6:15–16. It has dominated my thinking and praying ever since I saw it, strengthening my faith and increasing my thanksgiving. It keeps reminding me that God oversees the events that influence my life—even the happenings and contacts that seem to occur by chance.

It gives me fresh, thankful confidence that He is at work behind the scenes, always seeking to enrich me through each situation that comes my way. This truth helps my attitudes and reactions. It especially helps in relating to people who, intentionally or not, inconvenience me, resist me, or make demands that seem unreasonable. This brings special joy to my heart, because being gracious and thankful is often hard for me.

What an encouragement the passage has become:

> God, who is the blessed controller of all things, the king over all kings and the master of all masters . . . To him be acknowledged all honour and power for ever, amen! (1 Tim. 6:15–16, Phi).

Charles Swindoll calls the sovereignty of God the Christian's security blanket. His sovereignty assures us that our lives are under His guidance and care. Our circumstances lie within His sovereign purposes for us, whether by His immediate screening of events or by His basic intent to let us face and overcome what is common to humankind. Our joys and trials are permitted or arranged by the blessed Controller of all things, who is determined to bless us in all the situations of all our days. C.H. Welch wrote:

> The Lord may not definitely have planned that this should overtake me, but He has most certainly permitted it. Therefore, though it were an attack of an enemy, by the time it reaches me, it has the Lord's permission, and therefore all is well. He will make it work together with all life's experiences for good.[4]

As trusting and obedient children of the sovereign God, we can thank Him that we are not vulnerable or helpless. Under His protection and provision we can confidently give thanks for the blessing and growth that He will bring through whatever comes our way.

In his commentary on First Thessalonians, R.C.H. Lenski wrote:

> We need to learn this secret of the happy Christian life—thankfulness. If everything actually conspires to do us good, how can we do otherwise than always rejoice? What if we do not always at once see and feel the good, is there not joy in anticipating the sight?

4 Charles H. Welch, source unknown.

> The Christmas tree is already being decorated although the doors are still closed, yet how the little hearts beat with expectant joy![5]

Thanksgiving helps us anticipate the final unfolding of the delights our sovereign God has in store for us, as well as the multitudes of lesser joys He strews like flowers along our earthly path.

The Holy Spirit's Empowering

But we will never give thanks continually apart from being filled continually with the Holy Spirit. We need not persuade the Spirit to fill us, for He is most eager to do so. We just need to let Him. This is as easy as letting air into our lungs when we breathe. But as preparation we must sense our need and give the Spirit access to our entire life. If our heart is filled with our own ways or preferences, we restrict Him. He cannot fill what we reserve for ourselves.

AW. Tozer wrote:

> Before you can be filled with the Spirit you must desire to be filled. . . . Are you sure that you want to be possessed by a spirit other than your own? . . . That Spirit, if He ever possesses you, will be the Lord of your life! . . .
>
> That you want His benefits, I know. I take that for granted. But do you want to be possessed by Him? Do you want to hand the keys of your soul over to the Holy Spirit?[6]

As we let the Spirit fill us by simple, trustful yielding, He empowers us to do what we cannot possibly do on our own. He expands our hearts and enables us to enjoy the resources that are ours in Christ. He opens our eyes to the benefits, both present

---

5 R.C.H. Lenski, *The Interpretation of Sf. Paul's Epistles to the Colossians, to the Thessalonians, to Timothy, to Titus and to Philemon* (Minneapolis: Augsburg, 1964), 358.

6 A.W. Tozer, *How to Be Filled with the Holy Spirit* (Harrisburg, Pa.: Christian Publications, Inc., n.d.), 42–43.

and ultimate, that our heavenly Father intends to bring about through our circumstances. Then, through Him, we give thanks, identifying with David's confidence in Psalm 23:6, "Surely goodness and lovingkindness will follow me all the days of my life, and I will dwell in the house of the LORD forever."

For Personal Meditation and Group Discussion

1. Briefly state the two positions on the giving-thanks-for-all-things issue.

2. Why can we give thanks always, regardless of what happens?

3. Why is continual thanksgiving important?

11

Resolving Our Struggles

SHOULD PRAISE and thanksgiving be our first response to everything that happens?

Or, to resolve our struggles in depth, do we also—and at times, first—need to deal with our questions and our disturbed feelings?

Not all Christians agree in answering these questions. Some can readily resolve their struggles and restore their emotional equilibrium simply by praising or giving thanks. Others insist that often praise alone is not enough. In their opinion, praise can be a superficial solution, ignoring inner conflicts rather than solving them.

The man who wrote Psalm 73 struggled with serious misgivings. Why did corrupt and unjust men prosper while he, who lived an upright life, suffered day after day? He wrestled with this question intensely but quietly, not broadcasting his doubts and sowing seeds of distrust in other people's hearts.

After struggling in vain to understand, he decided to spend some time with God. There in His presence he saw things from a broad, eternal point of view. This settled his questions. He confessed that he had reacted as an animal, without spiritual understanding, until he brought God into his conflict. Then he began to praise God, declaring that He was more important than anything else in heaven or on earth. This psalmist was a man of praise, but praise was not necessarily his immediate or only response. He also gave honest thought to his questions and brought them to God.

Not A Quick Cure-All

The Bible does not teach that we should experience only positive feelings. It does not teach us to ignore our unpleasant emotions. If we fail to consciously experience our griefs, they can remain unresolved. The same is true if we deny our resentments or sweep our fears under some mental rug. They again—and often soon—reappear to distort our thinking and misguide our choices. So to disregard our distressful feelings and mask them with words of praise is not wise. It is a bit like treating cancer with candy or a broken leg with Band-Aids.

Sometimes we must come to the end of ourselves before we seem able to open our emotional life to God or even to ourselves. For years a friend, whom we will call June, has faced recurring traumas and bitter disappointments. Distressful emotions repeatedly sweep over her soul, threatening to engulf her. I (Ruth) have long prayed that God would bring her out of her long winter into a springtime of trust and praise. But more groundwork has first been needed—more deep plowing to prepare the soil of her heart.

SOMETIMES WE MUST COME TO THE END OF OURSELVES BEFORE WE SEEM ABLE TO OPEN OUR EMOTIONAL LIFE TO GOD OR EVEN TO OURSELVES.

Some months ago June reached new depths of despair, the sort of depression that could have led to suicide. God used this time of anguish to break through with the first warm breezes of springtime. Since then June has enjoyed occasional glimpses of sunlight shining through the dark clouds in her heart.

It seems that often I long to speed up processes that cannot be condensed to fit my timetable. Years ago, after careful prayer and thought, I urged June to seek release through praise. I encouraged her to base her praise on rich truths that she had enjoyed earlier but could no longer grasp emotionally.

My suggestion was premature, and on that day I was insensitive to her need for a shoulder to cry on. Longing to see her released, I was too eager to help free her through praise. I was like the man who saw a large butterfly struggling to force its body through one end of its cocoon. Concerned about the long, traumatic struggle, the observer took a pair of scissors and carefully snipped the cocoon, making the opening larger. The butterfly slipped out easily and quickly, but its wings never became strong and beautiful. The birth struggle was necessary, not optional, to its development.

Since those first faint spring breezes in June's life, progress is still slow. But she has reached the point where now and then, usually through music, she can crawl along the road of praise. I look to God, with thanksgiving, for the day when June will run along that road, but I have learned new lessons in patience. I am more prayerful lest my eagerness to help others should run ahead of God's timetable.

God's Healing Process

Yet praise has the potential of hastening God's deep healing process within us. How can this happen? We can take our cue from the psalmists. They knew how to mingle their praises with tears. When a psalmist expressed his troubles in prayer, he let God into his experience, choosing not to suffer alone or rely on his own limited resources. And when he praised, he revitalized his faith by focusing on God and His sufficiency.

King David is an excellent model. He repeatedly opens himself to God, both honestly and worshipfully. In many psalms he verbalizes his disturbed thoughts and feelings to the Lord. As he does so, he mingles his expressions of distress with words that honor God and affirm David's confidence in God's unfailing help.

In Psalm 25 David extols the Lord as good and upright, a guide to the humble, always loving and faithful to those who obey Him. Then he prays for God to be gracious in the midst of his loneliness, affliction, and multiplied troubles of the heart.

In Psalm 69 David has wept until he is exhausted. He beseeches God that the floodwaters, though up to his neck, will not engulf him. As he prays he repeatedly honors God in the ways he addresses Him: "O Lord, the LORD Almighty . . . in your great love, O God, / answer me with your sure salvation" (69:6, 13, NIV). He goes on to speak of the goodness of God's love and of His great mercy. Then he says, "I will praise God's name in song / and glorify him with thanksgiving . . . The LORD hears the needy. . . . Let heaven and earth praise him, / the seas and all that move in them, / for God will save Zion / and rebuild the cities of Judah" (69:30, 33–35, NIV).

David composed Psalm 142 when he was hiding from Saul in the cave. In this psalm he pours out to the Lord his complaint and his trouble as he looks to the right and the left and finds no one who cares for his life. Crying to God in his desperate need, he acknowledges God's sufficiency: "You are my refuge, / my portion in the land of the living" (142:5, NIV). Later in the psalm he prays that God will set him free from his prison so that he may praise His name in the congregation. He closes his prayer with confidence that God will answer: "Then the righteous will gather about me / because of your goodness to me" (142:7, NIV).

In instance after instance David demonstrates a constructive way of facing trials. He freely expresses his emotions to God, affirms his confidence in God, and speaks of God's positive qualities. He anticipates fresh reasons for praise when God's help will ultimately but surely come. Through honest prayer coupled with praise, David overcomes his discouragement and fear. He turns dangers, distresses, and malicious opposition into triumphs.

These examples show us a powerful kind of therapy: praise and thanksgiving coupled with honest expression of our thoughts and feelings. In our major struggles we can spend special time alone with God (and perhaps with a mature friend), letting ourselves feel what we feel and sharing our feelings honestly. Then we can offer praise, choosing to trust and honor the Lord whether or not we feel appreciative. We can continue to praise as we go on our way. In our lesser daily skirmishes we can praise God on the spot in our busy situations and later talk over with Him any negative feelings that still need resolving.

This blending of praise and honest expression of our feelings helps us experience our emotions without drowning in them. The tight knots within us loosen. Our questions about how God handles our affairs are settled, though at times they remain unanswered. We learn to trust Him in spite of gaps in our understanding.

> **BLENDING PRAISE WITH HONEST EXPRESSION OF OUR FEELINGS HELPS US EXPERIENCE OUR EMOTIONS WITHOUT DROWNING IN THEM.**

Some years ago I (Ruth) made friends with a woman who had lost her teenage son in a tragic road accident. Though years had passed, she had not yet resolved her grief. Her mind was still preoccupied with the loss, and little things would trigger fresh remorse—things like going into his bedroom or seeing an attractive young man the age her son would be had he lived. The mention of a sports event would cause her to mourn over what her son was missing. Invariably her conversations would swing back to that tragic focus of her heart.

Two things led to her inner healing. First, a wise counselor helped her recognize and express the immense hostility she felt—hostility about the accident, its loss to her, and its waste of a promising young life. Second, she saw her need to accept the accident and change her thought patterns. Again and again she chose to center her thoughts on the love and wisdom of God. She knew He could have intervened had it seemed best to Him, for "whatever the Lord pleases, He does" (Ps. 135:6). If He did not intervene, it was by wise and loving choice.

She refreshed her mind with God's commitment to cause all things to work together for good to those who love Him. And she began to turn her attention from her earthly loss to her son's unspeakable gain in a realm more real than the visible world and infinitely more exciting. She thought of him in heaven, totally fulfilled.

Fortified with these new thought patterns, she began to thank God. Later she told me in a stirring letter that now she was actually thanking God for taking her son home through the accident. This had helped resolve her grief.

Singing to the Lord

Much of the praise in Old Testament times was expressed in music and singing. The New Testament also encourages us to sing psalms, hymns, and spiritual songs, making music in our hearts to the Lord (Eph. 5:19). Always a great aid to worship and praise, music is especially important for us to use in times of inner turmoil or depression. When Ruth lived in Taiwan, a missionary wife told her, "If you hear me singing heartily, it may not be because I feel joyful. When I'm down, I find great relief in singing aloud to the Lord."

Listening to praise music also helps. We have a number of cassettes we like to use in praise during our quiet time, while we exercise or when we take walks. Often we use earphones in order not to disturb others.[1]

Recently we visited with a friend who serves the Lord in the Middle East. He described the immense blessings he has enjoyed through a fresh emphasis on praise. On past furloughs his months in the U.S. have been hectic, leaving him drained emotionally. During his recent furlough he decided to major on praise. Each morning in his quiet time he listened to praise music, singing along, raising his hands, freely expressing his delight that "our God reigns." Then he interlaced his prayer time with praise, which enabled him to pray from the perspective of the greatness of God and the richness of His resources. As our friend prayed about a need or a person, he would call on God's character and attributes, vivid in his mind through praise.

This friend is excited about the value of a heavy emphasis on praise. He says, "It helps me see and enjoy reality rather than be overwhelmed with appearances as they crash in on me. It has uncorked my emotions and motivated me afresh to memorize God's Word out of renewed love for the Lord." His worship now resembles wide-screen technicolor rather than black-and-white silent movies. He has returned to the Middle East excited about God and refreshed even after a busy furlough.

A Sacrifice of Praise

Hebrews 13:15 exhorts us to offer God a continual sacrifice of praise. This passage was originally addressed to people facing perplexity and impending danger. At times we can all identify with how these Christians must have felt. Our hearts feel disappointed

---

1 You can find excellent praise and worship music online or in Christian bookstores. In seeking to broaden your praise, try listening to an unfamiliar song several times before deciding it is not for you. This practice has brought us enrichment through songs and types of singing that initially did not appeal to us.

or overwhelmed, familiar emotional supports vanish, or we suffer failure, bereavement, depression. These times present to us the privilege of offering God a sacrifice of praise that costs us something. If we let our emotions control our responses to Him, we miss our opportunity.

Instead we can honestly express our feelings to God and then choose to give thanks. By doing this we prepare our hearts for release from the tyranny of our distressful emotions. We displace unbelief with faith, and false thought patterns with scriptural ones. We replace our self-centered reactions with attitudes that honor God. Again and again this allows God to fill us with His healing love. It opens the way for Him to deliver us, as He has said, "He who sacrifices thank offerings honors me, and he prepares the way so that I may show him the salvation of God" (Ps. 50:23).

For Personal Meditation and Group Discussion

1. Along with our praise and thanksgiving, what else can help resolve our emotional struggles?

2. Why might praise and thanksgiving alone be insufficient?

3. Is there some situation in your life, past or present, in which you can apply the therapy described in this chapter?

12

Using Trials for Good

WHY DOES GOD want us to give thanks always? Is it because all things are good? Surely not. Some things are evil, utterly contrary to the will of God, who delights in lovingkindness, justice, and righteousness (Jer. 9:24). But in the lives of His children God promises to cause all things to work together for good. God will make every happening serve His good purposes, both in our lives and in the world. As we commit our distressing circumstances to Him with obedient trust, they will become blessings. Therefore we can thank God regardless of what happens.

God's Refining Process

God uses trials in our lives to refine, beautify, and strengthen us. In our natural state our personalities resemble unrefined gold. The heat of our difficult circumstances melts the gold and brings to the surface the dross in our characters—the pride and unbelief, the unloving attitudes, the self-will.

Praising God brings our hearts in line with His intentions, so that He can work in us more freely. It opens us to His will, so that we can cooperate with Him in His plan to remove the impurities.

Yet, instead of praising, we so easily complain and resist His working. We blame others rather than asking the Lord to change us, regardless of who is right and who is wrong. By our complaints and resistance we stir the scum back into our personalities. This may necessitate the heat of continued chastening to accomplish what God wants to do in us. It may delay His answers to our prayers for both ourselves and our loved ones. In contrast, praise and thanksgiving can serve as catalysts, speeding up the refining process in our lives.

Praising God brings our hearts in line with His intentions, so that He can work in us more freely.

God seeks to refine us even through the trials, both large and small, that we bring upon ourselves. Warren and I often pray about various habits and reactions that, if unchanged, could become more ugly as age advances. We include such things as my bent toward anxiety, Warren's occasional critical spirit and reactions of anger, and our mutual tendency to interrupt others in conversation.

Recently we added my unwarranted inclination to feel anxious at times in Asian traffic and to offer reminders that border on backseat driving. This rarely bothers Warren. In fact, he repeatedly thanks me for my navigational tips. Yet I feel that change is in order lest I become a full-fledged backseat driver as I get older.

One morning we were zipping along Singapore's Bukit Timah Road to the Botanic Gardens for an extended time of prayer when once again I offered a backseat suggestion. A few moments later Warren graciously but firmly asked why I find it difficult to relax and trust his decisions. As we discussed this, I felt far from thankful. I sat there wrestling with a bit of self-justification and a lot of discouragement. On Monday I had decided that I wanted to change in this area, and now on Wednesday I had failed again! *Why, Lord?* I wondered.

As I prayed for insight, a basic cause of my problem became clear. I had allowed myself to feel personally responsible for Warren's driving, instead of entrusting it to him and to the Lord. I thanked God for giving me this deeper awareness, for now I could deal with a major root of the problem. I could refuse to interfere unnecessarily in a department of life that is not mine. I thanked the Lord that He was working to relieve me of my false sense of responsibility and that this day's incident was part of the process. I also gave thanks for Warren's gentle rebuke and for his excellent record as a driver. How gracious the Lord is to improve my life even through my self-induced trials!

God uses trials to perfect faith as well as character. Again and again trials bring us to the end of our human resources, so that we allow God to meet our needs and satisfy our longings. Trials rip away the flimsy fabric of our self-sufficiency. This allows God to weave into our hearts His strength, love, and wisdom. Trials exercise our faith, developing a strong confidence that says, "I am ready for anything and equal to anything through Him Who infuses inner strength into me [that is, I am self-sufficient in Christ's sufficiency]" (Phil. 4:13, AMP).

With God no problem in our personalities or circumstances is impossible or even difficult. Our troubles never surprise Him. They never catch Him off guard, causing Him to wring His hands and wonder what to do. As we repeatedly focus on God's sufficiency in difficult situations, we develop a steady trust in Him.

Choosing God's Perspective

In the late 1960s, we lived in the shadow of a low foothill that loomed up behind our house, completely blocking our view of Colorado's inspiring Pikes Peak. Sometimes we would get into our Volkswagen and drive to the other side of the city. There we could feast our eyes on Pikes Peak, which rose high and majestic, so overshadowing our foothill that we could scarcely locate it.

In a similar way praise helps us to stand back from our difficulties and fix our attention on our infinite, loving God. It helps us measure our problems against His limitless power, and suddenly the problems look like molehills rather than mountains. In the light of God's sovereign kindness and wise purposes, we see them as stepping stones rather than stumbling blocks, as opportunities rather than obstacles. They are the raw material for God's miracles and the prelude to greater obedience.

As our perspective changes, our feelings often shift from negative to neutral to positive. But even if they are slow to respond, we can continue to give thanks with our minds and wills. We can choose to rejoice that God is our source of wise guidance and overcoming power though we still feel angry or confused about our circumstances.

For some years we have been praying that a person very dear to us would be able to feel the warmth of God's love. Some time ago this person went through a kaleidoscope of trials, including a rather serious accident, some financial reverses, and a painful disappointment. "Surely," my (Ruth's) faltering faith told me, "all this will bring the opposite of what we have prayed." I began to mull over my complaint, asking, "Lord, when are You going to answer?" The moment I did so, the thought came strongly, "This is part of the answer." As I thanked God that He could use those trials to hasten the answer to our prayers, my anxieties fled.

In the days that followed, I thanked God repeatedly that He is all-wise and in control. This helped me to view the situation from God's perspective. It kept my heart steady. And God is continuing to answer our prayer for this person we love.

Overcoming Contrary Inclinations

"But," you say, "I simply cannot thank God in regard to certain things that have happened to me. I could mouth the words, but I wouldn't mean them." Probably we all feel this way at times.

And God has provided for the times when we are overwhelmed or perplexed or bitter.

God has given us His Word to reassure our hearts. Through it He reminds us of His loving goodness, which always plans for our best, of His wisdom, which never makes a mistake, and of His power, which can make something glorious out of the sorriest fragments of our lives.

God has also given us His Spirit, who energizes us to obey His command to give thanks. As we choose to thank Him simply because we want to obey and please Him, we switch on His power by faith. We give Him the opportunity to work in us, making us both willing and able to give sincere thanks in spite of contrary feelings.

> **As we choose to thank Him simply because we want to obey and please Him, we switch on His power by faith.**

By natural temperament we may differ from one another in the time that elapses between an event and our choice to give thanks, or between that choice and our upsurge of joy. As we focus on appropriate Scriptures and depend on the Holy Spirit, we can shorten our periods of inner resistance or adjustment. This is growth. Growth does not mean that we have no struggles, but that we more quickly resolve our inner conflicts.

One night the wife of Don Burns, a close friend who serves with Wycliffe Bible Translators in South America, suffered a sudden, totally unexpected heart attack. The doctor predicted that the attack would either take her life or leave her like a vegetable. Don was overwhelmed. Then he remembered that he and his wife had been developing the habit of thanking God for everything. Don could not bring himself to give thanks for his wife's heart attack, so he began by giving thanks for other things: the love they had for each other, the years they had enjoyed as a couple, their four delightful children, the honor of serving the Lord.

As Don praised and gave thanks for a multitude of blessings and happy memories, God's presence warmed and reassured his heart. Eventually he was able to thank God for his wife's critical illness. He also gave thanks for whatever outcome would most glorify God, whether life as a vegetable, physical healing, or the greater and total deliverance of departing to be with Christ. To Dan's delight, God completely restored his wife and has given them many years of continued service together.

Thanksgiving can help deliver us from the mental maze of analyzing again and again what happened, trying to figure out who is to blame, and reviewing the ways other people have mistreated us. It can free us from vain speculations on precisely how each circumstance could be part of God's sovereign will for our lives. Through giving thanks we put our stamp of approval on God's intention to use the trial for good. We do this not because we understand the specific whats and whys and hows, but because we trust His love and wisdom.

We endorse Paul's words in Romans 11:33–34 (PHI):

> I stand amazed at the fathomless wealth of God's wisdom and God's knowledge. How could man ever understand his reasons for action, or explain his methods of working?

When we give thanks although we do not understand, we stop trying to make God answerable to us for what He does or permits. We humble ourselves under His mighty hand and open ourselves to His grace.

Welcoming Trials as Friends

Through thanksgiving we obey God's command, "When all kinds of trials and temptations crowd into your lives, my brothers, don't resent them as intruders, but welcome them as friends!"

(James 1:2, PHI). James reminds us that trials come to test our faith. They develop us so that we will in no way be deficient. In view of these tremendous benefits, we are to welcome trials as friends. The King James Version says that we should count it all joy when we "fall into" many trials. A friend who often clarifies truth through homely expressions says, "We are to count it all joy when we fall in, not when we climb out!"

This attitude of accepting trials with joy was a principle with the Apostle Paul. He refused to lose heart when afflicted in every way, perplexed, persecuted, and struck down. He accepted these troubles as opportunities to manifest the life of Jesus to other people (2 Cor. 4:8–11).

Paul was committed to Christ's glorious purposes, regardless of the cost to himself in emotional struggles, intellectual perplexity, and physical pain or privation. His attitude was, "I will stand with God and the gospel, though I may stand with tears in my eyes, scars on my body, confusion in my mind, distress in my heart. I will align myself with this marvelous Person and His breathtaking purposes, and I will bless the Lord."

To maintain a similar attitude, I (Ruth) find it helps to have my true goals clearly set and to keep them in the forefront of my mind: to know God better, to love Him more, to glorify Him and do His will, to be conformed to the image of His Son. Then when I feel disappointed or distressed, I can waste less time in fleshly reactions. Instead, I can review my goals and then say, "This trial comes to fulfill my chosen goals, even though it frustrates my surface desires. Therefore I welcome it."

Using Everything for Good

Paul told the Corinthian Christians, "All things belong to you, whether Paul or Apollos or Cephas or the world or life or death or things present or things to come; all things belong to you, and you belong to Christ; and Christ belongs to God" (1 Cor.

3:21–23). In what way do all things belong to us? Perhaps in one of the ways that they belong to God: "All things are Thy servants" (Ps. 119:91). All things can be our servants. They are ours to use for good and for God's glory.

Early in his Christian life, E. Stanley Jones discovered the principle of using all things for good. He immediately began to make it a central and driving force in his life. He learned not just to bear opposition and difficulties in a passive manner but rather to actively use everything that happened, whether good, bad, or indifferent. When he was 83 years old he wrote:

> Make everything serve. Just as an airplane always rises from an airport, not with the wind, but in face of the wind, so I would make oppositions send me up, not down. . . . I could make things make me when they were intended to destroy me. . . .
>
> Jesus took the worst thing that could happen to him, namely, the cross, and turned it into the best thing that could happen to humanity, namely, its redemption. He didn't bear the cross; he used it. The cross was sin, and he turned it into the healing of sin; the cross was hate, and he turned it into a revelation of love; the cross was man at his worst, and Jesus turned it into God at his redemptive best.
>
> The answer, then, is: don't bear trouble, use it. . . . Take whatever happens—justice and injustice, pleasure and pain, compliment and criticism—take it up into the purpose of your life and make something out of it. Turn it into a testimony. Don't explain evil; exploit evil; make it serve you. Just as the lotus flower reaches down and takes up the mud and mire into the purposes of its life and produces the lotus flower out of them, so you are to take whatever happens and make something out of it.[1]

We serve a God who can cause all things to work together for good, both for ourselves and others. He can produce beauty out

---

1 E. Stanley Jones, *A Song of Ascents* (Nashville: Abingdon, 1979), 36–37,180–181.

of ashes, power out of weakness, growth out of failure, triumph out of distress. As we give thanks regardless of what happens, we align ourselves with God and His purposes. This prepares us to co-labor with Him in using for good the worst that happens to us in a fallen world.

For Personal Meditation and Group Discussion

1. Jot down some of the benefits of trials.
2. List some reasons why giving thanks in trials is important.
3. What in this chapter do you find most helpful for your own life?

Part III

Freedom

The rewards of worship are not a bouquet of roses promised if we do well. They are more like roses unfolding on the bush. The rewards are an intrinsic part of worship—intimacy with God, increased inner harmony, strengthened faith, conformity to His image, and service that stimulates others to worship as well as to serve Him. Such rewards gratify us. But supremely they gratify God, making His eternal longings come true.

The following chapters can lead us into the glad liberation that comes when we worship God as our highest treasure and open ourselves to greater intimacy with Him.

13

Joining the Treasure Hunt

WHEN JESUS HEALED ten lepers, He was disappointed that only one remembered to give thanks and glorify God (Luke 17:11–19). Psalm 106 shows how grieved God was that the Israelites seldom remembered His acts of lovingkindness. They preferred to grumble rather than to praise. When they did offer praise, as following the dramatic Red Sea deliverance, they quickly forgot what God had done and despised His abundant provisions. All they could think of was their intense craving for what they did not have (Ps. 106:12–14). In contrast, we can bring God pleasure rather than grief by remembering to thank and praise Him for what He does, what He gives, and what He is.

Expanding Our Praise

Even children can begin the adventure of praise and thanksgiving when inspired by parents, leaders at church, children's praise cassettes or records, and most of all the indwelling Holy Spirit. I remember as a young girl wholeheartedly singing praises in church and sitting alone at home worshipping God. Mother had taught me to kneel by my bed and silently pray each night, and somewhere—perhaps from my parents, perhaps from church—I had caught the idea of including praise in my praying. One day I learned a new, high-sounding word, "magnificent." Much impressed, I remember it that night as I knelt to pray, saying to the Lord, "You are magnificent!" Only God heard it, and I imagine He was pleased.

After Jesus had ridden triumphantly into Jerusalem on the first Palm Sunday, the children in the Temple praised Him. Jesus accepted their praise gladly. He quoted Psalm 8:2, "From the lips of children and infants you have ordained praise" (Matt. 21:16, NIV).

Children can praise God acceptably, as can new believers. But God desires growth in our praise that is consistent with our spiritual maturity. Is our garment of praise ample, or is it skimpy and outgrown-sleeves too short, too tight to button, seams ripping? Maybe even shrunk a bit?

GOD DESIRES GROWTH IN OUR PRAISE THAT IS CONSISTENT WITH OUR SPIRITUAL MATURITY.

In *The Christian in Complete Armour*, William Gurnall wrote:

> Now, as the coat you wore when you were a child would not become you now that you are a man; so neither will the garment of praise, which you clothed your soul with when a young convert, become you now that you are a mature disciple.[1]

Our praise and thanksgiving grow as we become more aware of who God is and of what He does, both in His overall providence and in direct answer to prayer. King David was alert to God and His works, always viewing Him as the source of all blessing and deliverance. Constantly David translated this awareness into words of praise and thanksgiving. We see this in Psalm 28:6–7:

---

1 William Gurnall, *The Christian in Complete Armour* (Glasgow: Blackie and Son, 1864), 458, archaisms removed.

Blessed be the LORD,
Because He has heard the voice of my supplication.
The LORD is my strength and my shield;
My heart trusts in Him, and I am helped;
Therefore my heart exults,
And with my song I shall thank Him.

To expand our praise and thanksgiving, we can set out on a treasure hunt, searching for new reasons for gratitude and admiration. Ronald Allen gives ideas for our search:

> Sometimes praise comes as the response to answered prayer; at other times praise is the result of meditation on the Scriptures that has led to a new insight into the wonder of the Lord. Praise may come from an ever-new sense of God's presence or a startling and dramatic sense of one's dependence upon His goodness.[2]

Allen also lists some of God's works that called forth praise in the psalms, including salvation, redemption, response to prayer, providence, protection, guidance, healing, sustaining, forgiving, satisfying. We can constantly find new reasons for praise as we seek to glorify God for what He does for us in every realm of life: physical and material, spiritual, intellectual, emotional, social, vocational.

We can also exalt the Lord for His awesome acts from the dawn of creation down through the ages—the mighty deliverances of His people; the wonder of Christ's coming to earth; the triumph of the cross; the glories of the Resurrection, the Ascension, and Pentecost; the rapid expansion of the church; the writing of the New Testament. We can praise God that His family has been growing throughout the centuries and throughout the earth. We can rejoice that He is constantly calling His children home to glory one by one, generation after generation. We can celebrate in

---

2 Ronald Barclay Allen, *Praise! A Matter of Life and Breath* (Nashville: Thomas Nelson, 1980), 16.

advance the day He will consummate all things in Christ, and we will be with Him forever as a vast family of brothers and sisters conformed to the likeness of His Son.

Psalm 111:2 says, "Great are the works of the LORD; they are studied by all who delight in them." The more we focus our attention on God's works, the more we will say with David and Isaiah:

> Many, O LORD my God,
> are the wonders you have done.
> The things you planned for us no
> one can recount to you;
> were I to speak and tell of them,
> they would be too many to declare. (40:5, NIV)

> O LORD, you are my God;
> I will exalt you and praise your name,
> for in perfect faithfulness
> you have done marvelous things,
> things planned long ago. (Isa. 25:1, NIV)

Pursuing God Himself

God delights in our praise for His works, but He also wants us to focus on who He is. Who He is and what He does are intricately related. One is the spring, the other the river; one the lamp, the other the rays of light. He expresses what He is in what He does.

God is the Savior, and He gives salvation. He is the Bread of Life, and He nourishes our inner person. He is generous, and He bestows good gifts. He is love, and He constantly demonstrates His love through attentiveness and protection. His acts flow out of who He is. Through His Word He reveals who He is, and through His deeds He confirms this in our personal experience.

God's works and gifts can enlarge and enrich our praise for Him as a person, or they can become idols that distract us from worshipping Him. God wants us to look beyond His blessings to Him as the Blesser, beyond His deliverances to Him as the Deliverer. He loves to act on our behalf. But to Him, that is just one part of a treasured personal relationship with us as our Father, Friend, and Bridegroom, our Shepherd and our King.

God wants us to look beyond His blessings to Him as the Blesser, beyond His deliverances to Him as the Deliverer.

God wants us to rejoice not just in His provisions but also in Him. He does not mind if we say, "I thank You," when we might better have said, "I praise You," as long as we express both gratefulness for what He gives and admiration for who He is.

As we pursue and appreciate God Himself and not just His benefits, we discover that He meets needs far deeper than His acts alone could ever reach. A.B. Simpson, founder of the Christian and Missionary Alliance, wrote:

> Once it was the blessing,
> Now it is the Lord.
> Once it was the feeling,
> Now it is His Word.
>
> Once His gifts I wanted,
> Now the Giver own.
> Once I sought for healing,
> Now Himself alone.[3]

God intends that all through life we should seek and enjoy His gifts and deliverances. Taking care of us is part of His role as our God. But He wants us, above all, to pursue Him for Himself. Tozer says that "the man who has God for His treasure has all things in

3 A.B. Simpson, "Once It Was the Blessing," from *Sacred Songs and Solos*, (London: Marshall, Morgan and Scott, n.d.), 593.

One. . . . Having the Source of all things he has in One all satisfaction, all pleasure, all delight . . . and he has it . . . forever."[4]

God seeks to win from us a deeper love through both His Word and His works. Through them He prompts us to praise Him for who He is as well as for what He does. He motivates us to exult in Him as the Supreme Ruler of all and to rest in the warm realization that this God is our God. This God of power, wisdom, and steadfast love, who is better than life and all it offers—He is our God forever. He is worthy of our highest praise.

Taking Action

We do not grow in praise merely by thinking that praise is a nice idea, one that we would like to act on once we get through our present time squeeze. Nor do we grow in this area by lecturing ourselves, "You should praise more," or by merely deciding to praise. We grow in praise by taking action—present-tense action.

We can begin by alerting ourselves to things that call forth the response of praise. Right now, without much deliberation, you could probably write down an inspiring list of wonderful works and divine attributes for which to praise God. Since praise is a response, meditating on such a list could touch your heart and help you praise. Then you could embark on a personal treasure hunt, daily observing and recording fresh reasons for praise.

For some years when I was a widow I kept a notebook on God. In one section I recorded what He does—His past, present, and promised actions. I wrote out verses that reminded me of wondrous things He did in biblical times, the amazing benefits He brought into my life through Christ, and His promises that He will meet all my earthly needs. In the other section I concentrated on who He is as revealed in His names, His titles, and His attributes (His love, grace, holiness, majesty, sovereignty, etc.),

---

4 A.W. Tozer, *The Pursuit of God*, (Harrisburg, Pa: Christian Publications, Inc., 1948), 20.

and on who He is to me as my Father, my Husband, my Light, my Life, my Refuge.

The section on who He is and who He is to me filled most of my notebook. One by one I added new pages as I made discoveries in the Word, reserving a full page for each attribute, name, and relationship that came to my attention. At the top of each page I wrote the topic. Then on the front I recorded verses or phrases of Scripture through which the Spirit clearly touched my heart. On this side I wanted nothing but the powerful Word of the living God, the authoritative description of what He has revealed Himself to be. On the back of the page I wrote my own thoughts about the Scriptures recorded on the front, plus quotes or poems on the subject and references of verses I wanted to consider later. I frequently added new verses, especially during my quiet time.

Often in times of need I would go back to one of the pages and let God refresh and reassure me. Even a page that had only one or two verses could meet my need and stimulate praise.

Thirsting For God

Whatever methods we use, increasing our knowledge of God can enrich us and our worship. Our worship, in turn, can produce in us a greater thirst to know Christ better.

When our granddaughter Kristen was seventeen months old, we soon discovered during a visit that she had one word regarding everything she enjoyed: "More!" Keen enjoyment calls forth the desire for more—more of the same. Worship brings a growing satisfaction with the Lord and a healthy dissatisfaction with our meager experience of Him. It helps to wean us from lesser cravings, focusing our affections on the One who alone is altogether desirable. E. Stanley Jones wrote, "I looked into His face and was forever spoiled for anything that was unlike Him."[5]

5 E. Stanley Jones, *Song of Ascents* (Nashville: Abingdon, 1979), 28.

The knowledge of God stretches before us like a vast, shoreless, bottomless ocean. We are all like children playing on the beach, enjoying the cool breezes and the breaking of the waves as we wade in the shallows. We launch deeper into His fullness by pursuing the knowledge of Him and taking time to extol Him for who He is and for what He does.

For Personal Meditation and Group Discussion

1. Make a list of significant events and blessings in your life, past and present, for which you want to praise and give thanks.
2. List five or six truths about God that you most appreciate. Have a time of worship, praise, and thanksgiving for both of these lists.
3. Decide on a plan for consistently recording truths about God that will enrich your worship.

14

Cultivating Joy

WHEN YOU HEAR the word *joy*, what comes to mind? Happiness? Laughter? Fun? The satisfaction of being promoted, of passing an examination, of owning a new Mercedes? The delight of spending Christmas with people you love?

Earthly joys can serve as reminders to offer thanksgiving and praise to God, "who richly supplies us with all things to enjoy" (1 Tim. 6:17). But as motivation for a consistent lifestyle of praise and thanksgiving, we need more than earthly joys. We need a deep, restful joy that does not depend on how well life is running. Though we should not wait for joyful feelings before we offer praise, God often uses joy to ignite appreciation in our hearts. If our praise remains only mind and will with no warm enjoyment, we may eventually lose heart and give up.

Experiencing God's Joy

The joy God gives far exceeds human joys. David could say, "Thou has put gladness in my heart, more than when their grain and new wine abound (Ps. 4:7). David's God-given joy surpassed the peak of human joy in his society, that of a bountiful harvest. The joy God gives is indescribable and full of glory. It surpasses human joy as a river surpasses the trickle from a faucet. It is the joy Jesus spoke of in John 15:11: "These things

I have spoken to you, that My joy may be in you, and that your joy may be full."

We are not implying that human joy is wrong. The Bible says that "a joyful heart is good medicine" (Prov. 17:22). A person with a fun-loving spirit, a lively sense of humor or a sanguine nature is one of God's special gifts to the human race. Natural joys are part of God's design for our well-being. They are meant to be the foam on our cup of deeper joy and the icing on our cake of spiritual gladness. Viewed as such, earthly joys contribute to our praise: Praise in turn keeps our joys God-centered. But if we praise only when we experience earthly blessings or feelings of exuberance, our praise will be shallow and intermittent.

EARTHLY JOYS CONTRIBUTE TO OUR PRAISE:
PRAISE IN TURN KEEPS OUR JOYS GOD-CENTERED.

The Israelites often came before God with shallow joy and shallow praise. When they saw God act on their behalf, they believed His words and sang His praises. Then "they quickly forgot His works; they did not wait for His counsel, but craved intensely in the wilderness, and tempted God in the desert" (Ps. 106:13–14). These people tested God instead of trusting Him. Their loyalty was like a morning cloud and like the dew which disappears early (Hos. 6:4). Their praise was like a plant that springs up quickly but has no deep root. Most of the time the weeds of unbelief and a complaining spirit choked praise in their lives.

How easy it is to be wholly absorbed with natural joys, or even with superficial excitement in praise. Would we settle for artificial orchids if we could have an endless supply of real ones? Would we cultivate dandelions, bright and pretty though they be, if we could grow roses and lilies? Probably not. Yet how often we fill our inner garden with lesser joys and longings, leaving little room for God's joy to bloom.

Asking for Joy

To be deeply joyful is Christlike. Jesus was anointed with the oil of gladness above His fellow men and came to replace our mourning with this same anointing of gladness (Ps. 45:7, Isa. 61:3). Even as He faced the cross, our Lord told His disciples that He wanted them to share His joy. The joy God gives is our birthright as His children. It is a fruit His Spirit wants to produce in our lives. Therefore we can expectantly ask God to increase our joy.

In Psalm 90:14 Moses prayed for an increase of joy based on God and His love: "O satisfy us in the morning with Thy steadfast love, that we may rejoice and be glad all our days" (RSV). And Paul prayed that the Colossian Christians would give thanks joyfully. We can pray the same for ourselves, asking God to increase our joy as we appreciate more fully His wonderful Person and ways.

It is not selfish to ask God for His joy, because the joy of the Lord gives us strength to do His will. Asking for joy is not asking for an easy life. The joy God gives does not banish all suffering or sadness from our lives. Instead it undergirds us in the midst of sorrow.

Some years ago I (Warren) heard of a godly Christian who had lost his daughter in a tragic accident. One day when out walking, he came to a street sign with her name on it. As grief and tears filled his heart, in an unexplainable way God's joy also flooded in, causing him to rejoice in the midst of his grief. He experienced what Paul meant when he described himself as "sorrowful yet always rejoicing" (2 Cor. 6:10).

If we lack God's joy in our lives, we can bring this need to God in prayer day by day. We can do this with confident expectancy, for Jesus said, "Ask and keep on asking, and it shall be given you" (Luke 11:9, AMP).

As we ask for joy, we should not set a time limit on God or dictate the process through which He will answer. Before the flowers of joy can bloom in our hearts, plowing, watering, and weeding are often necessary. We may need drought times, when our earthly wells run dry and we thirst for God in new ways. We may need disappointments that press us to partake of God's comfort or troubles that drive us to depend on His love and power.

Someone has written, "Sorrows come to stretch out spaces in the heart for joy." Even in the midst of my saddest bereavements I (Ruth) have found this true. The grief has turned me anew to God as my primary focus and source of joy. It has attuned my senses not only to God Himself but also to tiny natural delights, such as a look of joy on a child's face or a tree starkly silhouetted against a wintry sky.

In the alchemy of sorrow, natural joys and God's joy somehow fuse together in new ways. And as the process goes on, distress gradually enlarges our capacity so that we can contain more joy.

Jesus was anointed with the oil of joy because He loved righteousness and hated wickedness (Ps. 45:7). For us, too, actively loving what is right and hating what is evil is a taproot of joy. As we become more Christlike in this, we cast off hindrances to joy. Therefore we should not be surprised if the answer to our prayer for joy requires God's discipline, for such discipline increases our love for righteousness.

Often the answers to our prayers do not come through passive waiting for God to act. We must be alert to choices He wants us to make. We can pray for joy with confidence if we pray with a teachable heart:

> Lord, I ask for an abundance of Your joy in my life. I thank You that You will give it in Your perfect time, when You have prepared me for it. Guide me to any choices I must make or any actions I must take to make joy possible. Enable me to walk uprightly and to wait patiently so that this good gift, as well as a thousand others, may be mine.

A Byproduct of Knowing God

Joy can be defined as "pleasure or delight caused by something good or satisfying." We may profess to want God's joy and pray for it regularly. Yet we may actually be seeking joy that is based on variables—on people or possessions, on happenings or achievements that are short-lived and subject to change.

> **THE DEEP JOY OF GOD COMES TO HEARTS THAT VALUE HIM MORE THAN THEY VALUE ANYTHING ELSE, INCLUDING JOY.**

Until we set our sights on joy that is based on God and His will, we postpone indefinitely the day when we will know true, consistent joy, joy that does not fluctuate with happenings. Only God is always good and permanently satisfying. Everything about Him is unchanging and eternal—His love, His power, His throne, His promises. His joy expresses itself in a variety of forms—in restful enjoyment, carefree cheerfulness, jubilant exultation, or quiet expectancy of future delights promised in God's Word. Though the form may vary, the joy can never be quenched.

We prepare ourselves for this joy by choosing God as our primary source of joy and by fitting in with His purposes for our lives. Only as we fulfill God's design in creating us can we know true joy.

The deep joy of God comes to hearts that value Him more than they value anything else, including joy. A songwriter exemplified this God-first attitude when she wrote:

> My goal is God Himself, not joy, nor peace,
> Nor even blessing, but Himself, my God:
> 'Tis His to lead me there, not mine, but His—
> "At any cost, dear Lord, by any road!"[1]

---

1 Frances Brook, "My Goal Is God" (hymn), public domain.

The exiled psalmist who wrote Psalm 43 also maintained the heart attitude that is a prerequisite for joy. He valued God as His supreme satisfaction, speaking of "God my exceeding joy" though at the time his soul was downcast and disturbed (Ps. 43:4). He had developed a settled frame of mind that focused, even during times of distress, on the one unchanging basis for joy.

Paul considered everything as mere rubbish, worth less than nothing, compared with the priceless privilege of knowing Christ better. No wonder Paul was a man full of God's joy in spite of incredible hardships and sufferings. He exhorted his spiritual children to be joyful in the Lord, and he modeled God-centered joy at all times: in prison, in prayer, in relationships, in want, in plenty.

In Psalm 87 God's people declared that all their springs of joy were in Jerusalem, the city God had chosen as His special place to reveal Himself. His people found joy in Jerusalem because of the Person who dwelt there. But since the time of Jesus' death and resurrection, God is no longer associated with a specific earthly location. We who belong to Him do not rejoice in a place but a Person who reveals Himself to us anywhere as we seek Him. How appropriate for us to affirm to our Triune God Himself, "All my springs of joy are in you" (Ps. 87:7).

Because our springs of joy are in God, we can increase our joy by pursuing a deeper knowledge of Him. Among the truths that give rise to joy are God's total forgiveness, His unfailing love, His sufficiency, His faithfulness, and His ultimate victory in which we will share. As we focus on such truths, they strengthen our experience of God and help dispel emotions that suppress joy, such as guilt, anxiety, fear, resentment.

Drinking From Our Springs of Joy

We can drink from our springs of joy by praising God as we meditate on Him. King David pondered God's glorious reality and loving nearness. Then he wrote in Psalm 63:5–6, "My mouth offers praises with joyful lips. When I remember Thee on my bed, I meditate on Thee in the night watches." As we fill our minds with who God is, we trust Him more, and trust is a basis of rejoicing. Psalm 33:21 says, "Our heart *rejoices* in Him, / *because we trust* in His holy name." Truly believing the truths God has revealed about Himself enables us to drink of Him who is our joy.

As we reflect on who God is, we begin to sense who we are as His loved ones. We see ourselves as we are in Christ, blessed with inner springs of joy through the indwelling Holy Spirit. God has made us one with Himself, having given us His nature when we were born of Him. This spiritual birth has connected us with His everlasting joy.

We do not have to search for God's joy; it is already our possession, waiting for us to choose it above lesser joys. Our inner experience may drift in and out of this joy, but always the joy is there, waiting for new opportunities to flood our whole being. It is ours to settle down in.

Whatever our present feelings, we can begin praising God that we are partakers of Him—Father, Son, and Holy Spirit—and so are united with all His qualities: everlasting life and love, everlasting light and glory, everlasting joy. This union makes us participants in eternity now. We possess within us a down payment of the everlasting joy in which we will revel forever. This gives us unchangeable reasons to say with God's prophet of old, "I will rejoice greatly in the LORD, / My soul will exult in my God" (Isa. 61:10).

The Mark of Maturity

To experience God's joy consistently, we also need to make mature, obedient choices in our daily attitudes. One such choice is to rejoice: "Rejoice in the Lord always; again I will say, rejoice!" (Phil. 4:4). Many of us have fallen into the trap of postponing joy until our situation improves, our pain diminishes, our partner changes his or her ways, or our fortunes take a turn for the better. We feel we cannot rejoice while in our present circumstances. God disagrees. He says we should find our joy in Him at all times.

God also says we are to "count it all joy" when we meet trials. Rather than being enemies of joy, trials are signposts that can point us toward true joy. By depriving us of natural sources of joy, they remind us to choose God's joy. God uses trials to awaken us from the anesthetic spell of the world, which keeps us grasping for scraps of earthly joy and blinds us to the joy that awaits us in the Lord. We can postpone joy if we wish. But God invites us to rejoice in Him now. As we choose to do so, He supplies the power we need. The choice is ours alone.

GOD USES TRIALS TO AWAKEN US FROM THE ANESTHETIC SPELL OF THE WORLD, WHICH KEEPS US GRASPING FOR SCRAPS OF EARTHLY JOY AND BLINDS US TO THE JOY THAT AWAITS US IN THE LORD.

Another mature choice we can make is to adopt an attitude of hope—of expectant confidence regarding the future, based on the promises of God. Often the things we experience seem far from joyful. Jesus Himself was not filled with joyful exuberance as He suffered in Gethsemane and on the cross. But for the sake of the joy that awaited Him in the future, He thought nothing of the shame (Heb. 12:2). He endured with hope. Choosing a hopeful outlook can help us keep on rejoicing in the Lord regardless of what our natural feelings tell us.

So, whatever happens, we are to choose an attitude of rejoicing and hope. This choice hinges on a more basic choice—on simply deciding to believe God. In Romans 15:13 Paul says that as we believe, the Holy Spirit fills us with joy and peace, so that we may overflow with hope. The· Christians Peter wrote to experienced this: "Without seeing him you believe in him and so are already filled with a joy so glorious that it cannot be described" (1 Pet. 1:8, NJB). A missionary wife in China described this joy:

> Lord, I belong here at Your side,
> Singing Your song, swinging Your stride,
> Joy surging with the strength of a tide.[2]

In *The Ultimate Intention*, DeVern Fromke wrote:

> Joy is the one thing most evident in those who have been caught by the heavenly way and purpose of life. They have learned to live in the strength and source of JOY Himself. . . . We are called to joy. It is not optional but imperative that everyone who runs to win should exhibit joy, the mark of maturity.[3]

God is the rich soil in which joyful praise grows. At times, even early in our walk with Him, we may experience excited joy and delight. But as our roots go deeper into Christ, He captivates our thoughts and emotions in new ways. This makes our joy more full and stable. Then our praise can flourish, lifting its fragrance to God in every condition or season of life.

For Personal Meditation and Group Discussion

1. Why is it important to experience God's joy?
2. What truths about joy in this chapter most help you?
3. What things can you do if you would like to experience God's joy more constantly? What one thing can you begin immediately?

---

2 DeVem F. Fromke, *The Ultimate Intention* (Fort Washington, PA: Christian Literature Crusade, 1963, 1980), 115.

3 Fromke, 112.

15

Communing with God

OUR GOD IS A DELIGHTFUL Person. Sovereign, glorious, absolute in purity and power, He is also a God who delights in personal relationships. Never has He been a solitary figure, alone in an empty eternity. He is the Triune God; and throughout eternity the Father, Son, and Holy Spirit have related in unbounded intimacy.

By creating us in His image, God has destined us to be relational beings like Himself. Through our union with Christ He has welcomed us into His inner circle of triune love. He longs to enjoy unbounded fellowship with each of us.

Enjoying God's Presence

As we relate to people, we communicate on a variety of levels. We greet one another and talk about facts: the weather, our health, how the children are doing. Sometimes we venture a bit closer, sharing our ideas and opinions. With some people we dare to share our feelings, often with a degree of caution. Now and then we experience totally free communicating—a deep, uninhibited sharing of thoughts and feelings that could be called communion. This gives us glimpses into the other person that we miss in less intimate levels of communicating.

With God we can communicate on all levels. Even a "good morning, Father" can be meaningful. But with Him as with people, how often do we get beyond facts, beyond the business at hand, into the feeling level? And beyond that into unreserved spiritual communion? In communion we consciously relate to God in the deeper levels of our being. We pray and praise in our spirit, either with words or with wordless love, delight, concern, groaning, longing. We respond to God and His Word with heart as well as mind.

Although communion can be connected with thoughts about God, it also goes beyond thoughts into direct enjoyment of Him as a Person. Through it we can learn to delight in God as did F.W. Faber, the noted Victorian hymn writer:

> Only to sit and think of God,
> O what a joy it is!
> To think the thought, to breathe the Name,
> Earth has no higher bliss.[1]

ALTHOUGH COMMUNION CAN BE CONNECTED WITH THOUGHTS ABOUT GOD, IT ALSO GOES BEYOND THOUGHTS INTO DIRECT ENJOYMENT OF HIM AS A PERSON.

These lines convey the feeling of communion. Do we ever simply breathe the name "God" and let our whole inner being rest or exult in Him? Do we pause to worship or give thanks not only with our understanding but also with our innermost being?

Moses wrote, "Therefore know this day, and consider it in your heart, that the LORD Himself is God in heaven above and on the earth beneath; there is no other" (Deut. 4:39, NKJV). Psalm 46:10 is similar, "Be still, and know that I am God" (NKJV).

---

1 Frederick W. Faber, "My Father" (hymn), quoted in A.W. Tozer, *The Knowledge of the Holy* (San Francisco: Harper and Row, n.d.), 20.

God asks us to give careful thought to truths He has revealed about Himself. He also wants us to pause quietly before Him, to relax our hearts and minds and muscles, and to realize in the depths of our being that He is God—the one true God who rules over heaven and earth, the God of unfailing love who is always available to help us. In communion we take time to be still and enjoy this incomparable God.

Our communion can take many forms. It can be prayer punctuated with moments of silent reflection. It can be wordless awe as we read of God's power and creative genius. It may flood our hearts as we see a dawn or a sunset or a tiny flower boldly proclaiming God's glory. It may come as an upsurge of adoration at some simple reminder of our glorious Creator and King.

Communion may take the form of quiet receptiveness to God—a simple openness like that of the earth as it receives dew. It may resemble the silence of strong roots drawing up nourishment from well-watered soil. Through such silence we pause in restful dependence to enjoy fellowship with the Lord and draw on His sufficiency.

Praise and communion make ideal partners. Communion makes our praise more vital, less likely to be routine and superficial. It helps us bless and thank God with our inmost being. And rich, heartfelt praise often blends with communion as we enjoy and adore our altogether desirable God.

The Primacy of Communion

Helen Morken, who through the years had a profound influence on me (Ruth), was a woman of the Word, a woman of prayer, a woman who communed with God. One day as I visited with her, Helen remarked, "Everyone is talking about communication. But what about communion?" With God as with people, we may be experts in many kinds of communication, able to get thoughts across and present our case convincingly. Yet we may be unschooled in relaxed, personal fellowship with Him.

Although George Muller had walked closely with the Lord for sixteen years, when he was thirty-six he made a discovery that transformed his spiritual life. He described his new insight as follows:

> I saw more clearly than ever that the first great and primary business to which I ought to attend every day was to have my soul happy in the Lord. The first thing to be concerned about was not how much I might serve the Lord, or how I might glorify the Lord; but how I might get my soul into a happy state, and how my inner man might be nourished. For I might seek to set the truth before the unconverted, I might seek to benefit believers, I might seek to relieve the distressed, I might in other ways seek to behave myself as a child of God in this world; and yet, not being happy in the Lord, and not being nourished and strengthened in my inner man day by day, all this might not be attended to in a right spirit.
>
> Before this time my practice had been, at least for ten years previously as a habitual thing, to give myself to prayer after having dressed myself in the morning. Now, I saw that the most important thing I had to do was to give myself to the reading of the Word of God, and to meditation on it, that thus my heart might be comforted, encouraged, warned, reproved, instructed; and that *thus, by means of the Word of God, whilst meditating on it, my heart might be brought into experimental communion with the Lord.*[2]

Achieving or Communing?

As modern Christians, we find it difficult to pull ourselves away from our spiritual achieving to pause before God as a Person, quietly receptive. We find it easy to fill our quiet times to the brim with measurable activity and achievement, leaving little time for communion.

Could it be that we are too self-sufficient? Do we seek our deep emotional satisfaction in something other than God—perhaps even

2 H. Lincoln Wayland, ed. *Autobiography of George Miiller* (Grand Rapids: Baker, 1981), 206–207, italics added.

in reaching the goals we set for our spiritual intake or service? Or could it be that we feel more skilled, more safe, more comfortable in less personal relating? Both of us have noticed that sometimes at the point of keenest perception, at the breakthrough to communion, we suddenly get distracted by quiet time activities that seem more useful, or by the call of the practical.

> **TOO GREAT A FOCUS ON PERSONAL REQUESTS, OR EVEN INTERCESSION FOR OTHERS, CAN ROB US OF EXPERIENCING GOD IN INTIMATE FELLOWSHIP.**

Some of us miss communing by pressing to meet our goals in Bible reading, or we let prayer crowd out communion.[3] We persistently ask God to supply our needs, but we pay scant attention to His longings for us to enjoy His presence. In a recent letter Bob Sheffield, a leader in the U.S. Navigators, recently wrote:

> Under pressure I have begun to realize that my prayers seek the power of God and His strength, blessing, and refuge. It dawned on me that these are the outward manifestations of His Person. I began to see that at times I'm more drawn to seek His power and strength than His Presence! In the midst of the battle for survival I want His Presence more than His power.

Bringing our concerns to God in prayer is essential. But too great a focus on personal requests, or even intercession for others, can rob us of experiencing God in intimate fellowship.

In a busy or hurried quiet time we may meet the Lord in the less private rooms of our personality—in our mind, perhaps in our will, perhaps in the surface levels of our emotions. But most likely we fail to meet Him in the core of our being. His Spirit seeks to

---

3 We heartily advocate setting goals in reading the Scriptures. But all of our reading need not be done in our quiet times. We can set another time for finishing our reading, such as the noon hour or after dinner or sometime on Sunday. The same holds true for prayer.

warm our spirit with fellowship more intimate than even our closest human relationships can offer. If we neglect communion, we miss this basic ministry of the Holy Spirit in our lives.[4]

Some people, by nature or by culture, relate simply and intimately with others. For such persons communion with God may take place with little conscious attention. Not so with others. A small child who quiets himself in his mother's arms, absorbing her soft warmth and comfort, knows more about communion than many of us adults. We have lost our simple, childlike skills in intimate relating and have repressed our thirst for it. We need to learn how to respond with greater warmth and intimacy, both with people and with God.

In our early attempts to commune with God, we may feel so distracted, so unskilled that we decide this intimate relating is not for us. This is not because communion is complicated but because we are complicated, with our training in impersonal relating, our inverted values, our intense need to achieve, our fears of intimacy. Communion can help us shed our complexities and enjoy the simplicity of pure devotion to Christ. It can hasten us along the road of joyful obedience.

Learning to Commune

For many years, with occasional exceptions, my quiet times have been rich and profitable. I (Warren) have read the Word, prayerfully reflected on it, praised the Lord, and interceded. In recent years my enjoyment has intensified as I have given more attention to communion and developed greater skill in it. In the beginning of my daily times with the Lord, I remind Him that I am ready at any time to push back my scheduled procedures and pause to

4 Philippians 2:1 and Second Corinthians 13:14 speak ofthe fellowship of the Spirit. Our fellowship with the Father and with the Son is dependent on the Holy Spirit, who makes Their presence real to our entire being as we allow Him to do so.

commune with Him as long as He desires. Sometimes I secretly hope I will be able to complete at least my verse review and Bible reading before His invitation comes. To my momentary disappointment, He sometimes upsets my plans.

As I was reviewing my first verse one morning, He immediately focused my attention on the words, "We rest on thee" (2 Chron. 14:11, KJV). I took a few minutes to quietly enjoy Him as the One on whom I rely and rest. When I proceeded to the second verse, He again stopped me, this time with the statement, "Our eyes are upon thee" (2 Chron. 20:12, KJV). The Lord used these two brief sentences to initiate thirty minutes of delightful communion. I mentally sang the song, "We Rest on Thee, Our Shield and Our Defender,"[5] meditated on related verses, and enjoyed relaxed fellowship with Him.

My communion with God may be triggered by a verse, a phrase, a thought, a song. His invitation to intimate fellowship may come as a flood of light when He gives me new understanding of His Word. It may come as a warm sense of His everlasting arms holding and protecting me.

However the invitation comes, whatever inspires it, I must choose to pause and enjoy God with a quiet heart. I must refuse to press on with my scheduled reading or my prayer list or the duty that shouts for my attention. These can wait a while. A higher priority is to appreciate God in unhurried communion as I let my mind, my emotions, and my spirit experience Him.

Preparing Our Hearts

At times the Lord leads us into communion spontaneously, without conscious thought or planning on our part. This may happen on a busy street, during a church service, or in our quiet time. But often we must deliberately choose to cease from

5 Edith G. Cherry, "We Rest on Thee, Our Shield and Our Defender," from *Hymns* (Chicago: InterVarsity, 1960), 9.

our inner busyness and take definite steps to prepare our hearts for communion.

A good first step is to consciously depend on the Holy Spirit. He is within us to guide us into all truth. This guidance includes clear understanding of the Scriptures, but it includes more. The Spirit wants to lead us into experiencing the realities recorded in God's Word, and especially the realities of God Himself. Such experience often begins with mental enjoyment, but it is more than mental. Sometimes it is practical obedience; sometimes it is inner transformation, with or without our awareness. Sometimes it is simple communion as we enjoy God with heightened spiritual awareness. Our part is to ask for the Holy Spirit to lead us into communion with God and conformity to His ideal for us.

The Spirit wants to lead us into experiencing the realities recorded in God's Word, and especially the realities of God Himself.

We must also cultivate quiet receptiveness, which lets the Spirit infuse into our hearts living experience as well as accurate concepts. We can pray:

> Speak, Lord, in the stillness,
> While I wait on Thee;
> Hushed my heart to listen
> In expectancy.
>
> Speak, O blessed Master,
> In this quiet hour,
> Let me see Thy face, Lord,
> Feel Thy touch of power.[6]

Or we can use the song:

---

6 E. May Grimes, "The Quiet Hour," from *Inspiring Hymns*, compiled by Alfred B. Smith (Grand Rapids: Singspiration, 1951), 153.

Open my eyes, Lord,
I want to see Jesus,
To reach out and touch Him
And say that I love Him.
Open my ears, Lord,
And help me to listen.
Open my eyes, Lord,
I want to see Jesus.[7]

Sometimes praying for quietness and exposing ourselves to God's Word fully prepares us for communion. At other times distracting thoughts and concerns crowd into our minds. Rather than feel guilty about them, we can quietly and decisively put them aside. One by one we can place them on an imaginary shelf at our side or in the Lord's hand—that worry about passing an examination or finding a suitable job, that problem with our partner, that eagerness to see friends at a party next week, that thought of praying for someone. As we shelve each item, perhaps jotting it down as a reminder, we can say, "Lord, we'll talk about that later. Right now I want to enjoy communion with You."

Intimacy with God

Although communion primarily means enjoying God, it can include a wide range of emotions. We can commune with the Lord when we feel confused, sorrowful, even depressed. Whether or not we sense His presence emotionally, we can freely share our feelings with Him and open ourselves to His sufficiency. We can pray unhurriedly, with pauses to expose our hearts to Him more fully:

> Father, I'm hurting . . . I feel overwhelmed by this grief, this anxiety, this confusion . . . But You are my Father . . . my loving, compassionate Father . . . I turn my heart to You, for in

7 Bob Cull, "Open Our Eyes, Lord" from *Scripture in Song* (Maranatha! Music, 1976), Volume 2, No. 185, personalized.

> all my distresses You are distressed . . . and to Your Son, who is touched with the feeling of my weaknesses . . . and to the Holy Spirit, the blessed Comforter and Encourager . . . Thank You that I am not alone in my pain . . . You are with me . . . my Refuge . . . my strong and loving Shepherd . . . my ever-present help in trouble. I choose to trust you.[8]

We can commune with God regarding any feeling we experience, using it as a springboard to focus on Him as the answer to our deepest needs.

As obedient and cleansed children, our part in communion with the Lord is not to generate pleasant emotions. It is simply to turn our hearts to God as a Person, attentive to Him and caring about His longings to relate to each of us intimately. When enjoyable feelings elude us, we can pray, "Lord, I don't feel warm or worshipful, but I do love You, and I want close, personal fellowship with You. Free me emotionally as I continue to seek You day after day; Lead me into communion and worship that is rich with a sense of You."

Whether or not communion seems easy to us, whether or not we immediately enjoy it, God will enrich us as we take time to learn it through regular practice. We may need to persist for some time before we gain skill in relaxed enjoyment of His presence. We may need to repeatedly acknowledge our inadequacy and cast ourselves on Him. It may take prayerful effort, but the rewards will be great. As A.W. Tozer wrote:

> The fellowship of God is delightful beyond all telling. He communes with His redeemed ones in an easy, uninhibited fellowship that is restful and healing to the soul.[9]

---

8 This prayer is a paraphrase of the following verses: Isaiah 53:4; Hebrews 4:15; Isaiah 63:9; John 14:16, 26; Psalm 23:1, 46:1.

9 A.W. Tozer, *The Root of the Righteous* (Harrisburg, Pa.: Christian Publications, Inc., 1955), 121.

Listening

In the early years of our marriage Ruth sometimes felt I was not listening as she shared thoughts or feelings that were important to her. On one occasion I kept glancing through a magazine as she spoke. When she asked if I were listening, I repeated what she had said, point by point.

"Well," she said, "I still don feel that you heard me."

Though I could parrot what she had said, on a deeper level she was right. I had failed to get the pulse, the feeling, behind her words. I had not met her as a person, with the thoughtful attention that would have conveyed a caring interest and made her feel heard.

Is it possible that we think we are listening to God with open ears, yet fail to tune in to Him as a Person? Often we come to His Word and to prayer only halfway disengaged from other seemingly pressing pursuits. We come with our preconceived viewpoints, our distracting desires, our planned procedures—and we easily miss the truth He wants to convey. We settle for our immediate, superficial grasp of what the Lord says, inattentive to Him and His fuller illumination.

For some of us, seeking to listen in a new way as we come to the Word of God may be a good initial step in learning to commune with Him. First, we must recognize that it is possible to mentally enjoy truths, even truths about God Himself, and yet not fully feed on Him. He wants to nurture our entire inner person. This requires meditation and application, but they are not enough. It also requires that we absorb and assimilate truth through intimate fellowship with Him.

Often we are like a homemaker who prepares an elaborate buffet meal but never sits down to savor its rich flavors. She nibbles a bit as she cooks but misses the enjoyment and nourishment of the full feast. An attitude of quiet listening helps us relax in God's presence and enjoy His reality, His love, His power, His majesty. It prepares us to absorb His strength much as a sponge absorbs water or as the earth absorbs warm sunshine. Coupled with obedience, it enables us to assimilate God's beauty and sufficiency into the very fabric of our being.

Delighting in God Through His Word

God's written Word provides the ideal, always-available avenue to communion with Him. By meditating on a specific portion of Scripture, we can let its meaning enrich our understanding. Then we can go over the portion again with frequent pauses for silent reflection as we absorb its truth and fully delight in its Author. For example, we enjoy using Psalm 63:1, with appropriate pauses and repetitions:

> O God . . . Thou art my God . . . Thou art my God . . . I will seek You . . . I will seek You earnestly . . . My soul thirsts for You . . . My flesh longs for You in a dry and thirsty land, where there is no water.

Or we may simply say: "O God, You are my God," and find many moments of delight in this profound truth. Often we thoughtfully add our own responses:

> O God . . . You are my God . . . You have chosen me . . . and I have chosen You as my only God, my only Lord . . . We are committed to each other for eternity! . . . All around me is a dry, barren desert, offering nothing that can meet my deepest needs. . . . But You are more than sufficient . . . sufficient to satisfy my thirst . . . and to stabilize my emotions. Thank You . . . I love You . . . I praise and worship You!

Sometimes just the word "God" or "Father" or "Jesus," repeated with deep appreciation, is enough to bring us into intimate fellowship. Our goal is a very personal and unhurried response to God, uninterrupted by busy thoughts or diversions. God has filled His Word with windows that open into breathtaking, reassuring views of Him. Sometimes they are little windows of one phrase or even one word. Sometimes they are large windows—an entire verse or passage. Sometimes we can find new ones in our quiet times; at other times we can go back to old ones discovered yesterday or long ago.

God's written Word provides the ideal, always-available avenue to communion with Him.

We can take many of these views into our minds, reflect on them one at a time, and let their meaning enrich our understanding. We can build them into our hearts by praying over them and memorizing them. Then through communion we can feast on the views they offer of God and His ways. This turns our hearts from the hurried to the relaxing, from the ordinary to the uplifting, from the discouraging to the inspiring. It enables us to wait before God in relaxed silence as He strengthens us for the next obedient action. It lets Him fill us with the warmth of His presence that can influence our emotions and reactions all day long.

A Restful Center

God always is reaching out for intimate fellowship with us. He delights in the mutual enjoyment communion brings. He longs to fill our emptiness and fortify us for obedient living.

The more we cultivate the art of communion, the more our fundamental attitudes will change. Beneath the ebb and flow of our surface experience will run a strong current of calm joy in the Lord. From this restful, dynamic center will flow the power we need for a lifestyle of worship and obedience.

As we experience the Lord in intimate communion, we help Him fulfill the song:

Drop Thy soft dews of quietness
Till all our strivings cease.
Take from our souls the strain and stress
And let our ordered lives confess
The beauties of Thy peace.[10]

For Personal Meditation and Group Discussion

1. Describe communion and its benefits.

2. Which ideas about how to commune with God seem most helpful to you? Select one or two for immediate use in your quiet times.

10 John Greenleaf Whittier, "Dear Lord and Father of Mankind," from *The Book of Hymns* (Nashville: The United Methodist Publishing House, 1964), 235.

16

Enjoying Rich Benefits

MOST OF US HAVE A keen interest in bargains and good investments. We keep our eye on the ads in the newspaper and clip coupons that offer discounts. We look for a good deal when buying a car and a profit when selling one. Investors watch the stock market or the price of gold. Collectors search for rare stamps or coins. Some people simply dream of finding that pot of gold at the end of tomorrow's rainbow.

To motivate us in our spiritual lives, the Lord often appeals to our desire for profits and rewards. He promises abundant inner riches, practical blessings, and eternal enrichment as we seek Him and do His will. He says, "Those who honor Me I will honor" (1 Sam. 2:30). This promise applies to many things, including worship.

The most exciting material gains pale when you compare them with the riches that worship brings, both to us and to God. In this chapter we have gathered together various benefits of worship, many of them gleaned from earlier parts of this book.

Benefits to God

Our heavenly Father is not indifferent to our responses to Him. He seeks people who will truly worship Him; He urges us to praise Him; He declares that giving thanks is His will for us. He is grieved when we ignore Him, delighted when we worship Him.

As we worship in spirit and in truth, we minister directly to the Lord Himself, offering sacrifices of praise and thanksgiving that bring rejoicing to His heart. We give Him something unique, something no one else in the universe can give: our personal love and adoration. This deepens the intimacy He longs for and helps complete His joy in being our Father, our Beloved, our Friend. By giving Him the positive responses of our hearts, we actually add to His pleasure.

FAILURE TO PRAISE HIM THWARTS HIS GRACIOUS PURPOSES FOR US AND ROBS HIM OF GLORY THAT IS HIS DUE.

Not to worship God is injustice on our part. He is worthy to receive honor and glory and blessing, for "all things were created by him, and all things exist through him and for him" (Rom. 11:36, TEV). He is highly to be praised as our Maker and Sustainer, who supplies our needs out of His boundless resources. At great cost to Himself He has redeemed us, opening the way for us to come freely into His presence with our homage and gratitude. One of His purposes in redeeming us is that we may be to the praise of His glory, both through verbal praise and through our lives (Eph. 1:6). Failure to praise Him thwarts His gracious purposes for us and robs Him of glory that is His due.

Experiencing God

Besides bringing joy and glory to the living God, our worship enriches us. As spotlights accentuate the beauty of a painting or as sunshine highlights the brilliant hues of flowers, so worship and praise enhance our appreciation of God. They sharpen our spiritual perception for a clear, exciting look at His wonders. As we worship, God communicates His presence to us. He becomes more real to us. We honor Him, and He honors us with fresh manifestations of Himself.

This brings us a growing satisfaction with the Lord and a growing dissatisfaction with our meager experience of Him. Our thirst for Him increases, for to see Him is to desire Him. As worship weans us from lesser cravings, we find ourselves impelled to pursue Him more earnestly. As a cook watches for new recipes or an artist for new scenes to paint, so a worshipper searches out new reasons for gratitude and admiration. Because this centers our attention on God as we feed on His Word, it enlarges our knowledge of Him. It makes our enjoyment of Him more complete, our experience of Him more constant.

Worship is indispensable to full spiritual vitality and maturity. As we give it high priority day after day, the Lord deepens our ability to do what He most highly prizes: to love Him with all our heart, soul, mind, and strength.

An Undivided Heart

Worship and praise nurture within us a supreme desire to honor God. As this central longing grows, it focuses our energies and reins in our scattered interests. It directs our minds and hands and feet to do God's bidding.

A true and wholehearted worshipper develops a lifestyle of obedience to God. David, perhaps the greatest model of praise and thanksgiving in the Bible, poured out his praise to God in Psalm 40. Then he said, "I delight to do Thy will, O my God; Thy Law is within my heart" (Ps. 40:8).[1] As a man of the Word and of worship, David had bonded his heart to the will of God. The result—joyous obedience.

Richard Foster wrote in *Celebration of Discipline*,

> If worship does not propel us into greater obedience, it has not been worship. Just as worship begins in holy expectancy, it ends in holy obedience. Holy obedience saves worship from becoming an opiate, an escape from the pressing needs of modern life.

1 This verse is also a prophecy referring to Christ.

> Worship enables us to hear the call to service clearly so that we respond, "Here I am! Send me" (Isaiah 6:8).[2]

Worship also helps us keep our praying God-centered. Without it we are in danger of seeking God mainly to get what we want, be it possessions, health, human love, success, or fruitful service. We are also in danger of self-centered praise, through which we hope to obligate God to answer our requests. Genuine worship keeps God as our primary focus, with the things we want secondary. The prophet Habakkuk provides a moving example here. In a time of bitter disappointment he exalted God above his personal concerns and longings:

> Though the fig tree should not blossom,
> And there be no fruit on the vines,
> Though the yield of the olive should fail,
> And the fields produce no food,
> Though the flock should be cut off from the fold,
> And there be no cattle in the stalls,
> Yet I will exult in the LORD,
> I will rejoice in the God of my salvation. (Hab. 3:17–18)

A Powerful Therapy

The Bible does not present praise as a quick, easy cure for all our emotional conflicts and stresses. Yet when we couple praise and thanksgiving with honest prayer about our feelings and needs, they provide a powerful therapy. They dispel the darkness of our unbelief and melt our resistance to God. They serve as major stress reducers. They help release us from compulsiveness, from anxiety, and from a critical spirit toward other people. A.W. Tozer wrote,

> Thanksgiving has great curative power. The heart that is constantly overflowing with gratitude will be safe from those attacks

2 Richard Foster, *Celebration of Discipline* (San Francisco: Harper and Row, 1978), 148.

> of resentfulness and gloom that bother so many religious persons. A thankful heart cannot be cynical.[3]

Praise bears us up in suffering, bringing renewal as the Lord's presence enfolds us. In bright as well as gloomy days, praise and thanksgiving provide frequent mini-vacations that relax, refresh, and invigorate us.

Worship changes our view of ourselves. As we bow before our holy and glorious God, we realize how small and dependent we are, how prone to sin, how undeserving of His favor. At the same time, worship imparts to us a sense of significance as servants and loved ones of the Supreme Ruler of the universe. We deserve eternal separation from God and His glory, yet we are eternally united with Him through Christ. In our inmost being we are alive with Christ's life—His righteous, resurrected, triumphant life. Giving thanks for these truths deepens our joy in their reality. It nurtures within us a sense of who we are in God's estimation, producing a mysterious blend of humility and exaltation of spirit.

This God-centered sense of identity liberates us from self-absorption. It releases us from the craving for independent self-esteem that characterizes our day. It frees us from our false, easily threatened, natural sense of identity that gives rise to a multitude of evils.

Praise also changes our attitude toward circumstances. The thing that slowly poisons us is not our situation but our response to it. By promoting acceptance in place of grumbling and discontent, praise extracts the poison from our lives. It helps us view our difficulties as opportunities rather than obstacles. It brings a joyful anticipation of God's blessings, both the final unfolding of His glorious purposes and the favors He lavishes on us in the meantime.

3 A.W. Tozer, *The Root of the Righteous* (Harrisburg, PA: Christian Publications, Inc., 1955), 122.

So praise is therapeutic both in dispelling stressful emotions and in nurturing positive ones. It releases us from being submerged in visible realities and enables us to revel in the greater realities of God—His perfect attributes, His incomparable greatness, His sure promises, and the honor of fitting into His purposes.

BY PROMOTING ACCEPTANCE IN PLACE OF GRUMBLING AND DISCONTENT, PRAISE EXTRACTS THE POISON FROM OUR LIVES.

Growing Christlikeness

In Second Kings 17:15–16 we read that Israel forsook God to worship false gods: "They went after emptiness and became empty" (MLB). We too become like what we worship. Worship of the true God hastens our transformation into the image of Christ, for through it we expose our whole being to His influence. William Temple wrote:

> To worship is to quicken the conscience by the holiness of God, to feed the mind with the truth of God, to purge the imagination by the beauty of God, to open the heart to the love of God, to devote the will to the purpose of God.[4]

By focusing our hearts and minds on the Lord, worship shifts us from self-centeredness to Christ-centeredness. It brings us into line with His intentions, and it releases the transforming power of the Holy Spirit in our lives. It serves as a catalyst, speeding up the refining process in our characters.

As we worship the Triune God, His power and compassion increasingly permeate our lives. We become more able to love others with Christ's sacrificial love. Richard Foster says:

---

4 As quoted by Foster, 138.

> In worship an increased power steals its way into the heart sanctuary, an increased compassion grows in the soul. To worship is to change.[5]

To be transformed in character and attitude into the image of the Lord Jesus Christ—what higher reward could we ask? Gripped by the magnificence of this reward, E. Stanley Jones wrote:

> "Changed into his likeness." That is our destiny, and that is our reward! Was there ever such a destiny, and such a reward? Changed into the likeness of the most wonderful Character that ever lived upon this or any other planet—that is the highest and noblest destiny and reward that has been offered or can be imagined.[6]

Besides hastening our long-range transformation, praise is a regal garment that can daily beautify us as children of the King. It adorns us better than any other. We should not consider ourselves dressed in the morning until we have put it on.

Praise Brings Deliverance

Because worship helps us feed more fully on God, who is our highest good, it needs no external reward. Would we reward a hungry man for eating or a thirsty man for drinking? Not to worship is to deprive ourselves of a full experience of God.

Yet worship and praise often bring external as well as internal benefits. God does not promise that praise will usher us into a trouble-free utopia where all our dreams will come true. Yet as we enthrone Him in our situation through praise, we prepare the way for Him to meet our needs. We read in Psalm 68:4,

> Sing to God, sing praises to His name;
> Cast up a highway for Him who rides through the deserts,
> Whose name is the LORD, and exult before Him.

5 Foster, 148.

6 E. Stanley Jones, *Song of Ascents* (Nashville: Abingdon, 1979), 391.

The following verses of this psalm speak of those who are walking through. the various deserts of human experience—the fatherless, the widows, the lonely, the prisoners, the poor. God rides through these deserts, not to see the sights as a tourist, but to pour forth abundant, merciful rain, bringing relief to the needy.

This passage implies that praise plays a part in providing a highway for the Lord. Psalm 50:23 confirms this: "He who sacrifices thank offerings . . . prepares the way so that I may show him the salvation of God" (NIV). Through praise and thanksgiving we help build a smooth, level road on which the Lord can ride forth unhindered to bring deliverances and blessings.

Earlier we saw in Second Chronicles 20 that when the Israelites began to sing and to praise, the Lord utterly defeated their physical enemies. The same principle holds true in our spiritual battles. By prayer and praise we declare our trust in God to deliver; we lift up the shield of faith; we release the Holy Spirit's power. We make a frontal attack that can devastate Satan and his forces, for it calls into the battle God's dynamic presence. Prayer filled with praise can thwart Satan in our lives and in the lives of others. It can remove mountains of resistance that obstruct the Lord's pathway as He seeks to liberate and bless us.

When the early Christians met their first serious opposition, they turned to God in prayer that was largely praise. Acts 4:31 describes the result: "They were all filled with the Holy Spirit, and began to speak the word of God with boldness." Through prayer saturated with praise, the activities Satan wanted to stop advanced with renewed power.

By stimulating us to believe God, praise and thanksgiving often move God's mighty hand in solving problems and ending trials. At other times the specific blessings and deliverances we long for are delayed or withheld. Even then, praise and thanksgiving can have a powerful effect on us and, through us, on our situation. They transform our attitudes. They tune us in to the ways we can colabor with God in using our distressing circumstances creatively. They give fresh reality to our witnessing both by life and by word.

So one reason God seeks worship is that He desires to meet our needs, practical as well as spiritual. We worship to give to Him, to satisfy His longing for a deep relationship with us. He in turn pours benefits into our lives and situations. Can we ever out-give God?

Vitality in Serving

The most exciting external reward that worship offers is the special touch of God Himself on our service for Him. Worship prepares us for service that glows with God's presence. A.W. Tozer wrote,

> We're here to be worshipers first and workers only second. . . . The work done by a worshiper will have eternity in it.[7]

Worship infuses the glory of God into what we do and what we say for the Lord. It brings to our witness the freshness of the psalmist, whose heart was "bubbling over" with the good things he shared about the Lord.[8]

Service that does not flow from a worshipful relationship with God often becomes a rival of worship. One chronic temptation of devoted Christians is to rush around answering endless calls to minister to people, to the exclusion of ministering to our Lord Himself through worship. When we substitute service for worship, we make service an idol. This happens most easily in the use of our creative capacities and our most enjoyed spiritual gifts.

Apart from worship, service easily becomes half-hearted for some of us, compulsive for others. It degenerates into an uninspired grind of duties or an intense proving of ourselves through achievement. Do we want to be more than mediocre in the glory

---

7 AW. Tozer, *Gems from Tozer* (Send the Light Trust, 1969), 7.

8 Psalm 45:1; Roland Kenneth Harrison, *The Psalms for Today* (Grand Rapids: Zondervan, 1961).

we bring to God? Do we long to have an extraordinary influence in people's lives from His viewpoint, one with a supernatural touch? Then we must take time for worship as well as for serving. We must view worship as indispensable preparation for service.

When we substitute service for worship, we make service an idol.

However, worship is not the whole answer to effectiveness. We also need to saturate ourselves with God's Word, to intercede in prayer, to fellowship with other believers, and to share Christ with those who do not know Him. But worship is the peak of the pyramid, the summit of the mountain of spiritual living. Without worship we labor through days and years of spiritual mediocrity, offering God deficient service, even though people may admire our zeal, our eloquence, or our self-sacrifice.

Service that manifests the fragrance of Christ comes from those fortunate laborers who give worship a high place in their priorities.

Paul, as both a worshipper and a worker, could say that through him God spread the sweet aroma of the knowledge of Christ in every situation (2 Cor. 2:15). A.S. Wilson put it this way:

> Not merely in the words you say,
> Not only in your deeds confessed,
> But in the most unconscious way
> Is Christ expressed.
>
> . . . .
>
> To me, 'twas not the truth you taught,
> To you so clear, to me still dim,
> But when you came to me, you brought
> A sense of Him.
>
> And from your eyes He beckons me,
> And from your heart His love is shed,

Till I lose sight of you, and see
The Christ instead.[9]

Our Crowning Privilege

Rightly the benefits of worship motivate us. But the rewards of worship are not a bouquet of roses promised if we do well. They are more like roses unfolding on the bush. The rewards are an intrinsic part of worship—intimacy with God, increased inner harmony, strengthened faith, conformity to His image, and service that stimulates others to worship as well as to serve Him. Such rewards gratify us. But supremely they gratify God, making His eternal longings come true.

Although worship brings rewards, it is not primarily a means to rewards or fruitfulness or anything else. As one of the ultimates for which God designed us, it is not a path to other goals but a preview of our eternal destiny and reward.

Our crowning privilege is to worship God, simply because He is worthy.

For Personal Meditation and Group Discussion

1. List below the benefits of worship, praise, and thanksgiving that seem most significant.

2. Write several statements that motivate you to worship. (They can be quoted from the chapter or stated in your own words.)

3. Pray over the things you have written, asking the Lord to deeply motivate you to develop a lifestyle of worship, praise, and thanksgiving.

---

9 A.S. Wilson, "Indwelt," quoted by Isabel Kuhn in *Second Mile People* (Robesonia, Pa.: OMF Books, 1983), 35–36. (Other sources attribute this poem to Beatrice Cleland.)

Special Section

THIS SECTION CAN launch you more fully into the delights of worship as a lifestyle. These pages give you an opportunity to explore some captivating truths about our incomparable God and the privileges He has granted us.

For maximum profit, allow at least one day for each page. Begin by thoughtfully going over the day's portion of praise, lifting your heart to the Lord in worship, praise, and thanksgiving as you read. Add related thoughts of praise that come to mind—your personal reflections, verses of Scripture, songs on the subject. Give thanks for specific ways God has demonstrated the day's truth in your life and in the lives of others.

After your time of worship using the praise portion, go on to the study suggestion for that day. When Scripture references are given, pray that through them the Holy Spirit will open your eyes to see God more clearly. Use each verse as a basis for praise and thanksgiving, and then record your thoughts.

For further praise and thanksgiving throughout the day, select one statement from the praise portion or the Scriptures used. As an example, for Day 1 you might choose, "You hold in Your own power my breath of life and all my destiny," or simply, "my King and my God." To help establish a habit of frequent worship, use the statement or phrase in the morning, each time you give thanks for your food, and as your last thought at night. Jot down the references of verses that come to mind as you use the praise portion or do the study suggestion. If a verse speaks to you in a special way, copy it in a personalized form for future praise.

You might find it helpful to begin a worship notebook. In it you could record your answers to the questions in this section, as well as copies of the seven portions of praise. Both now and in the future, such a notebook could help you record and use Scripture portions, quotations, songs, and other aids to worship. As you use these pages repeatedly in your quiet time, they can continue to enrich your worship of our wonderful Triune God.

Day 1

My Majestic and Powerful King

My soul magnifies You, my King and my God,
for Your limitless power
and the glorious splendor of Your majesty.
You rule over the far reaches of the universe;
You are the unseen authority over all authorities.

I praise You for Your sovereignty
over the panorama of my life
and over each day.

"You hold in Your own power
my breath of life and all my destiny" (Dan. 5:23, MNT).[1]
You cause all things that come my way
to serve Your glorious purposes.

Thank You that I can face each tomorrow with confidence
because You hold the future.

The plans of Your heart will stand forever.

"Thine is the kingdom, and the power,
and the glory, forever. Amen." (Matt. 6:13)

As you go back over the above portion line by line, write in the space provided further thoughts of praise and thanksgiving to our majestic God.

1 Personalized.

Day 2

My Loving and Gracious Father

Thank You, Lord of heaven and earth,
for Your perfect love and abundant goodness.

You are gracious and compassionate,
full of lovingkindness, ready to forgive,
patiently considerate, and generous beyond imagining.

I rejoice that You have chosen me
and brought me near to You, to dwell in Your courts.

Thank You that You are my God, my King, my Friend,
my Refuge in trouble and danger,
my Father to care for me,
my Shepherd to guide,
my Bridegroom to delight in me.

"Because Thy lovingkindness is better than life,
my lips will praise Thee" (Ps. 63:3).

Consider the following Scriptures, and write your own paragraph of praise and worship to your heavenly Father: Luke 1:78–79 (a prophecy fulfilled when Jesus came), John 1:12–13, Ephesians 2:4–7, First John 3:1–2.

Day 3

My Exalted Lord and Savior

Thank You, Father,
that Your love surpasses all human loves.
By Your tender mercies our Lord Jesus
did not cling to His rights as Your equal
but emptied Himself of His privileges
and became man
and humbled Himself to die a criminal's death.

Thank You that You laid on Him
the crushing weight of all my guilt.
He became sin for me, dying the death I earned.

I praise You that You raised Him from the dead
and gave Him a position infinitely superior
to any conceivable government or ruler or power,
visible or invisible,
not only in this present world,
but also in the one to come.

I exult that He is able to save me completely
and present me faultless before Your glorious presence
with shouts of everlasting joy.

What else do you appreciate about Your Lord and Savior? Write down the things you think of and use them to worship Him.

Day 4

Holy Spirit, Gift from Above

Thank You, Father, Giver of every good and perfect gift,
for sending us the Counselor, the Spirit of truth,
to be with us and in us forever.

I rejoice that Your Spirit,
coequal with You and Your Son,
inspired the Holy Scriptures
as a light shining in a dark place.

Thank You that by Him a virgin conceived
and bore a Son,
and that Your Spirit rested upon Him,
anointing Him to bring good news
and to set captives free.

Thank You that the Spirit ministers to me as I trust You,
leading me on level ground,
enabling me to obey You,
filling me with love, and joy, and peace,
making my outlook radiant with hope.

Thank You that He has gifted me to serve You
and empowered me for spiritual warfare,
where victories are won not by might, nor by power,
but by Your Spirit.

Take time to write further thoughts of praise and thanksgiving for the Holy Spirit and His ministry in your life.

Day 5

My Indwelling Lord

How grateful I am, dear Father,
that Christ is my life
my resurrected, all-powerful, indestructible life.

I rejoice that He is able to untangle the snarls within me,
and replace old patterns of life with fresh new ones.
He is able to flush out my fleshly reactions—
my anxieties, my fears, my resentments, my regrets—
and fill me with the fruits of righteousness,
to Your glory and praise.

By Him I am able to do Your will.
I am ready for anything and equal to anything,
as I let Him infuse inner strength into me.

I give You praise,
for by Your power at work within me
You are able to do infinitely more
than I dare to ask or imagine.
I love You, Lord.

Consider the following Scriptures and write your own paragraph of praise and thanksgiving for what Christ came to do in you: Isaiah 61:3; Romans 6:4; Philippians 1:11, 2:13; Titus 2:14.

Day 6

My Treasury of Truth

What a treasure Your Word is to me!
I praise You for caring enough to communicate with us
in this written, always accessible way,
making Your truths available to water our souls
and accomplish Your purposes in our lives.

Thank You that in Your Word
I can hear Your voice and seek Your face
and perceive more clearly the wonders of Your Person.

There I can discern Your patterns for living
and learn to run the way of Your commandments
as You enlarge my heart.

Thank You that the Holy Spirit uses Your Word
to enlighten and bless me,
to guide and nourish and transform me.

Your words have become the joy and rejoicing of my heart,
for I am called by Your name, O Lord God of hosts.
(Jer. 15:16)

Meditate on the song on the next page, or another on this subject, and use it in prayer, praise, and thanksgiving.

Break Thou the bread of life,
Dear Lord, to me,
As Thou didst break the loaves
Beside the sea.
Beyond the sacred page,
I seek Thee, Lord.
My spirit pants for Thee,
O living Word.

Thou art the Bread of life,
Dear Lord, to me.
Thy holy Word the truth
That changes me.
Give me to eat and live
With Thee above,
Teach me to love Thy truth
For Thou art love.[2]

2 Mary A. Lathburg, "Break Thou the Bread of Life," from *Inspiring Hymns*, compiled by Alfred B. Smith (Grand Rapids: Singspiration, 1951), 99.

Day 7

My Free Access in Prayer

I praise You, glorious King of kings,
for granting me access into Your presence
just as I am, in Christ's merits, not my own.

To think that I can come right into Your presence
fearlessly, at any moment,
assured of Your glad welcome.

I can approach Your throne with fullest confidence
to receive mercy for my failures
and well-timed help for every need.

Thank You that You restore my soul
as I wait on You in quiet communion,
letting You enfold me with Your love,
absorbing Your strength and gladness.

I praise You that I can minister to others through prayer,
releasing in their lives and service
Your quiet, revolutionary, life-changing power.

Never has there been a God like You
who acts in behalf of the one who waits for Him (Isa. 64:4).

Consider Psalm 100, and use it for praising and worshipping the Lord. (If you would like, write it here in personalized form.)

Unbounded Unity

We adore Thee,
One God in persons three,
One God, one Majesty
There is no other God but Thee,
O blessed equal three,
Unbounded unity.[1]

1 Art Apgar, "We Adore Thee," from the cassette, *Because of Jesus* by Irene Trapp and Art Apgar, © 1983, Art Apgar, P.O. Box 95, Campbell, CA 95009.

Index of Scripture References

Also by Ruth and Warren Myers

Pray!

How to Be Effective in Prayer

"Lord, teach us to pray."

(Luke 11:1)

God loves when His people pray! But just how important is prayer in the life of a Christian? What should we pray about? Does God care how often we pray or what we pray for?

In this book, Warren and Ruth Myers teach us how to pray, outlining the biblical principles, patterns, and practices of prayer. They offer a rich theology of prayer, but also provide practical ways to enrich your prayer life. Whether shaping habits for your own quiet time or explaining the Lord's Prayer, Warren and Ruth use Scripture as the foundation for their teaching. They exhort all Christians to practice prayer, dependent on the help of the Holy Spirit, to intercede for the lost and support God's global mission.

Learn how to pray, whom to pray for, and why prayer matters.

Includes prayer-based tips for planning your quiet time

Size 5 1/4 x 8, Pages 211

ISBN: 978-1-61958-387-0

ISBN (*e-book*): 978-1-61958-388-7

THE NORMAL CHRISTIAN LIFE

. . . is Watchman Nee's great Christian classic unfolding the central theme of "Christ our Life." Nee reveals the secret of spiritual strength and vitality that should be the normal experience of every Christian.

Trade paper ISBN: 978-0-87508-990-4

THE NORMAL CHRISTIAN LIFE STUDY GUIDE

Gives a brief summary of each chapter of the book and then gives questions designed to provoke thought and possible discussion.

Trade paper ISBN: 978-1-61958-129-6